Love Letters
To a Child

Tracy Finck

TRACEY FINCK

Love Letters to a Child

A RESOURCE FOR PARENTS AND GRANDPARENTS

WINEPRESS **WP** PUBLISHING

WinePress Publishing (PO Box 428, Enumclaw, WA 98022) functions only as book publisher. As such, the ultimate design, content, editorial accuracy, and views expressed or implied in this work are those of the author.

ISBN 1-57921-838-5
Library of Congress Catalog Card Number: 2005910645

Dedication

This book is dedicated to
my children—Betsy, Britta, and Jack—who
have infinite patience with my parenting faults
and who inspire me with their boundless
love and enthusiasm for life.

Table of Contents

Acknowledgments ௦

I'm grateful to many people for having made my life—and this book—better than they could have otherwise been:

- My parents, Rev. Richard and Audrey Gilmore, for bringing me up in a household of love so that I would know how to create something similar for my own children.
- My father-in-law, Will Finck, whose faith and support made the entire project possible in many ways.
- My editor, Mary Lou Sather, whose encouragement and suggestions gave me fresh energy in the final stages of revision.
- My friends Beverly Johnston and Gabi Sutton, who read early drafts and offered helpful feedback.
- Generous people who shared journal entries: Cindy and Mark Wolbert, Teri Hyrkas, April Austin, Peggy Crooms, and Ruth Ann Kragt.
- Most of all, my best friend and husband, Greg Finck, who makes married life joyful and parenting fun (I don't say *easy*).

Proactive Parenting

God does not just want people to be saved from eternal damnation; He wants them to be transformed in every dimension of their earthly existence by the miracle of His grace. Children matter to God because He loves them and wants them to experience the best, right from the start of their lives. He relies upon us, their teachers and protectors, to deliver the guidance and experience they need to grow in their understanding of love for and obedience to Him.

—George Barna[1]

In 1994 Mary Pipher published the book *Reviving Ophelia: Saving the Selves of Adolescent Girls.*[2] I was writing a weekly parenting column for the local newspaper at the time and skimmed the book to try to find an answer to a question sent in by a reader. I found more than I was looking for.

---

[1] George Barna, *Transforming Children into Spiritual Giants* (Ventura, CA: Regal, 2003)

[2] Mary Pipher, Ph.D, *Reviving Ophelia: Saving the Selves of Adolescent Girls.* (New York: Random House, 1994). The excerpts here are from chapter 13: "What I've Learned from Listening."

The book presented a frightening picture of the effect American culture has on girls as they enter adolescence. It made me want to pack up my three little children and head for someplace safe—like the 1960s. The blurb on the front cover promised "an eye-opening look at the everyday dangers of being young and female, and how adults can help." As I read, I felt an increasing sense of urgency. My little girls were growing up quickly; soon they would have to pass through the danger zone. So was Jack, my baby—and I realized that as a boy he would have his own challenges and plenty of them. But there were things I could do to help my children survive.

Pipher encourages "the development of those qualities . . . found in all healthy families: appreciation and affection, commitment, positive communication, time together, spiritual well-being, and the ability to cope with stress and crises." My husband and I were committed to all these values as well as to praying for our children. And as Christians we had a coherent worldview to offer our children that could help them make sense of their experiences.

Twila Paris sings about "True North" as a metaphor for Truth. Pipher uses similar imagery when counseling confused teens: "You are in a boat that is being tossed around by the winds of the world. . . . True freedom has more to do with following the North Star than with going whichever way the wind blows. Sometimes it seems like freedom is blowing with the winds of the day, but that kind of freedom is really an illusion. It turns your boat in circles."

Proactive parents give their children room to think and discover things for themselves, but don't neglect their God-given role as guides. They don't hide wisdom from their kids. Nor do they fail to prepare them to meet life's challenges. Instead, they are intentional about introducing them to the God who made them and loves them and about instilling in them biblical principles and positive character qualities. This Goliath-sized challenge is apt to make any parent feel like David.

What we need is a sling-shot. Some simple and uncomplicated tool that can effectively get the job done—in the name of the Lord. There are perhaps many such tools, but the one I've discovered is something just about as disarming as a sling and a stone. It's a journal and a pen: I write love letters to my children—in the form of a journal.

My daughters are now seventeen and fifteen, and my son is twelve. When I look at them, I see three precious ships making their way heavenward—tossed a bit by the winds of culture, as all our children are—but fairly well on course spiritually and mentally and emotionally. The journals seem to serve as something of an anchor to steady them and a navigational map to help them understand where they are in life's journey.

PART I

SOWING THE SEEDS

Chapter 1

A Different Sort of Journal

> *Writing is a form of cherishing.*
>
> —Julia Cameron

Just for You

Imagine picking up a book, flipping through it, and finding to your surprise that it was written for you—literally. The author had you and only you in mind. It's as personal as a love letter. Flipping through the pages, you find a record of clever things you forgot you said, acts of kindness you committed over the years, details about what you used to do and the things you loved. All written by someone who sees you through the eyes of love and finds even your idiosyncrasies charming.

I write books like this for each of my three children. They are simply empty journals that I buy at a bookstore and keep close at hand so I can capture moments too valuable to forget. I write down interesting things my children say or do when they are at their best. Sometimes I include Scripture verses, bits of wisdom, quotations I've discovered, words from a song that my children love. I paste in photos that show off my favorite aspects of their character.

My original purpose in keeping these journals was to record my own experience of motherhood because I knew memory would fail me. I thought, too, that the journals would be a good legacy to leave my children. Since then, I've come to realize that the value of the journals is not only for the future.

Already the dividends have far exceeded the time I've invested. My children love these "Me & You" books and not only read them but also sometimes suggest things for me to write in them. The books are powerful bonds and give creative focus to my individual relationship with each child.

My oldest daughter, who is seventeen as I'm writing this, uses her book as soul food. The entries help her understand who she is as she makes her way into adulthood. One day she was sharing with me the difficulties some of her friends were having and telling me about their strained relationships with their parents. She said, "Too bad their moms don't write journals for them; it would help them so much. Mom, you should tell other moms that they should write journals for their kids."

Taking up her challenge, I began to use speaking opportunities to share the idea of writing journals for people we love. (Spouses, friends, parents, siblings or traveling companions might also be encouraged by a personal journal written exclusively for them by you.) Some people who were inspired to start writing have gotten back to me with reports like, "I started these books for my kids, and they are just eating it up!" One woman wrote to say, "The most exciting thing for me is using your idea of keeping a journal about each person in the house. Thank you for such a wonderful–rich–exciting–uplifting idea. I feel like I'm getting out of the parental humdrum into something meaningful."

I hope you will have a similar experience.

The Power of a Parent's Words on Paper

Mother Teresa was, for me, a role model of love. I recently watched a documentary about her life and learned something that amazed me. I had never heard this little fact before, but now it strikes me as one of the most significant details in her life story. It happened when she was thirty six years old and living in Calcutta as a nun, running a school. The convent was an oasis within the city, and the well-to-do families sent their children to that school. Mother Teresa was comfortable and happy.

Then one day, she received a letter from her mother. It said, "Remember that you went to India to serve the poor." Shortly after that, on the way to her annual retreat in the mountains, she heard God tell her to leave the comfort of the convent and live among the poor to serve them.

As I heard the narrator read these words, I caught my breath. To think of the significance of her mother's words—words written in ink on paper! That letter opened the door for the defining moment of Mother Teresa's life. Just to learn of it was something of an epiphany for me—and the journals I had been writing to my own children took on even greater significance. If even Mother Teresa profited by written messages from a parent, how much more do my children need my encouraging reminders to be all they can be?

It was in this same documentary film that I heard Mother Teresa describe herself as "a pencil in the hand of God." I've taken that metaphor as my personal motto. I want to be an instrument that God can use to influence my children for good.

That's my ideal.

The reality is that boredom, exhaustion, confusion, busyness, and chaos will crowd out meaningful moments whenever I let them. I can't totally eliminate those aspects of parenting, but I can move them into the background by focusing my attention on the gifts my children are to me, and the gifts I want to give to them. Journals help me do that.

Chapter 2

Putting Your Love on Paper

*If your lips can speak a word of encouragement
to a weary soul, you have a talent.*
—Eva J. Cummings

Remembering What We Want

Parents long to connect deeply with their children. To have a significant, positive impact on their lives. To celebrate their successes and discoveries and the ordinary moments of their daily lives. This isn't the experience of most parents. But it could be.

The problem is, we forget.

We get distracted, preoccupied, bulldozed, confused. We get tired.

We need something to remind us, to keep us awake. For me, the reminder is a book: an empty journal asking to be filled with evidence of a childhood properly enjoyed. Of life fully embraced. Of a relationship strongly rooted.

What this Book Is About

The idea is to keep a journal for someone as a gift of love. I do this for my children. I start with empty books—journals with blank pages. A separate book for each child. The entries are written to or about the person the journal is for. Some take the form of a love letter; some are quick descriptions of moments I want to remember or simply notes jotted down. Chapters 3 and 4 describe in detail the various types of entries I typically make. The great thing about a project like this is that it can be completely tailored to fit your individual style and application. You wouldn't need to use a bound journal. You could jot down your thoughts or a memorable line your child said on separate pieces of paper—scraps or napkins or whatever is close at hand—and keep them in a drawer or a file or a box. Or you could tape those scraps into a journal, as I do, to give the journal texture. My kids respond to my love letters like flowers to sunshine.

Here's an entry from my oldest daughter's book (Betsy was ten), in which I shared with her the purpose of the journal:

> From reading *The Horse and His Boy*[3] with you, I learned that we each eventually get to see the meaning of our own lives, but no one else's. We are told our own story and only our own story. No one can know another's story. And we often only learn our own after the fact.
>
> I keep this journal for you to help you piece together your own story. It's the greatest gift I can think of to give you—one of the greatest. I also want to give you myself and my time and good books and love and fun times: joy, adventure, opportunities.

---

[3] C. S. Lewis, one of the *Chronicles of Narnia*.

Unforgettable, Indubitable Love

Sometimes when I teach parenting workshops, I ask people to think back to their childhoods and identify things their parents did that made them feel loved. Sadly, some adults can't think of anything. They may know that their parents really did love them, but they can't think of special times when they really felt it emotionally. The problem may be one of different communication styles. In their book *The Five Love Languages of Children*,[4] Gary Chapman and Ross Campbell make the point that each person expresses and receives love best through one of five different communication styles. The five styles, or "love languages," are quality time, words of affirmation, gifts, acts of service, and physical touch. Just as people have different God-given personality types, they also favor different love languages. If a parent gives one type of love—say, a gift—but the child longs for a different expression of love—say, spending time together—then that child may not feel especially loved. All kinds of problems can spring from this, including insecurity, bitterness, resentment, even destructive behavior.

How can we be sure our children are able to receive the unconditional love we want to give them? Chapman and Campbell suggest two things. First, identify your child's primary love language. One way to do this is to notice what he or she does to express love to you and other people. Kids who color pictures for you or wrap up "treasures" to give you speak the language of gifts. If your kids give lots of hugs and frequently ask to cuddle, they use the language of physical touch. Children who tell you they love you and offer compliments speak the language of words of affirmation. The ones who try to help you or do favors for you use the language of acts of service. And kids who ask to accompany you whenever you run errands prefer the

---

[4] Gary Chapman, Ph.D., and Ross Campbell, M.D., *The Five Love Languages of Children* (Chicago: Northfield Publishers, 1997.)

language of quality time. If a child favors one of these, then be sure to express your love to that child with extra doses of that particular expression of love.

Second, realize that everyone needs all five expressions of love. You wouldn't withhold birthday presents from a child simply because "gifts" isn't his primary love language. Nor would you avoid hugging a child whose language isn't physical touch. The best way to convince our kids they are loved is to show them in all five ways. In fact, my experience is that by speaking all the love languages to all my children, I'm expanding their vocabularies and teaching them to be multilingual lovers. Of my three children, the one who most frequently and consistently reads and comments on her journal is Betsy, whose primary love language is quality time and whose secondary language is physical touch. At least that's what I thought when I first heard this concept years ago. But now I notice her using all five languages fluently, which is my goal for myself as well as my children.

Keeping a journal for your child is a powerful way to combine four of the five love languages—everything except physical touch. Children whose primary love language is words of affirmation will particularly thrive on the words you write in the journal. Children whose primary language is quality time will enjoy using the journal as a record of your times together. You can also spend time together reading through the journal and savoring happy memories. The book requires your time and effort and is certainly an act of service for your child. And of course you will eventually give the journal to your child as a gift. All children, no matter what their primary love language, will receive this as love.

Documenting Spiritual Milestones

Throughout the Bible, God tells people to remember. He created our minds and our memories, and expects us to use them.

Just before the Israelites are about to enter the Holy Land, after forty years of wandering in the desert, Moses gives a powerful speech. In it he stresses the importance of remembering: "Only be careful," he says, "and watch yourselves closely so that you do not forget the things your eyes have seen or let them slip from your heart as long as you live. Teach them to your children and to their children after them" (Deuteronomy 4:9).

Brent Curtis and John Eldredge address the weakness of our memories in their book *The Sacred Romance:* "The most crippling thing that besets the pilgrim heart is simply forgetfulness, or more accurately, the failure to remember."[5]

The failure to remember can lead to doubts, insecurities, loss of direction, and meaninglessness. To fortify your child's memory by recording key steps in his or her spiritual journey is to provide an anchor that may help your child survive coming storms of doubt or confusion. One very significant event to record is the moment your child first says yes to God. The following event took place when Betsy was five and is recorded in the first little book I kept for her:

12/17/93. We were driving to the babysitting co-op at church. You said something like, "Good thing I'm being good so Jesus will take me to heaven."

I tried to explain that no one can be good enough to get to heaven, but the way to get to heaven is to ask Jesus to live in your heart so He can forgive you when you're not good enough.

You said you wanted to pray and ask Jesus into your heart, so we did. Now you are a Christian and my prayer is answered.

All the angels in heaven are rejoicing to welcome Betsy into eternal life beginning now!

---

[5] Brent Curtis, and John Eldredge, *The Sacred Romance: Drawing Closer to the Heart of God* (Nashville: Thomas Nelson), 202.

On 9/16/96 I recorded this in Britta's book:

> Tonight you prayed spontaneously, "God, I give myself to You. I want You to be the ruler of me." I asked if this was the first time you've ever given yourself to God.
> Yes.
> I explained that you need to ask Christ to forgive your sins and trust Him to carry you to heaven.
> You do!
> We called Betsy and Daddy down to your bedroom and we all prayed together. Betsy said, "This is your Christian birthday." You asked if I could bake a cake for you to celebrate. Yes! I can have no greater joy than knowing I will enter the gates of heaven with my children by my side. I look forward to spending eternity with you, my bright shining star!

Jack's story is recorded only as the little speech he memorized to say at church when he was seven. (I can't believe I didn't record the actual event. The only excuse I can think of is that it was near the time we moved into the house we now live in. I must have been distracted. I hear you saying that you can relate.)

> 4/13/01. I became a Christian when I was four years old. One day I stole my sister's toy car, and I felt bad. My mom told me it was a sin, and only Jesus can forgive sins. She said I could ask Jesus to come into my heart and forgive all my sins. So I did. Now I'm a Christian.

Even small instances of spiritual growth can offer invaluable evidence that your child is truly being transformed by God's Spirit. Here's an entry from Britta's book:

> The kitchen is beautiful! All the dishes are washed, dried, and put away—in spite of the fact that the

dishwasher was full and running. You did it all by hand. Without being told to and without complaining!

When I asked about this miracle, you said that Jesus was in the kitchen with you and He told you to do it, just like the pastor talked about in church this morning. Wow. That's just about all I can say. Wow.[6]

Jesus said, "Anyone who loves me will obey my teaching. My Father will love them, and we will come to them and make our home with them" (John 14:23 TNIV). I can see that God lives in your heart, Britta. The beauty of the kitchen is just a little reflection of the beauty in your soul.

This is what life is all about: hearing God's voice and responding with cheerful obedience. I want her experience in the kitchen to be one of the defining moments for Britta. I want her to base her identity and self-concept on choices like that. So I record it in case her memory fails. Larry Christenson, in *The Christian Family*, says, "A child whose faith consists solely of a learned doctrine may have that faith badly shaken when it collides with rival doctrines in high school and college years. But a child who carries about within him the memory of countless encounters with the reality of God will not have to worry about holding his faith. His faith will hold him."

Rules for Getting Started

Rule #1: Only write what is true and positive.

If it's not positive, they won't read it. If it's not true, they won't trust you.

---

[6] This line is from *Lilly's Purple Plastic Purse* by Kevin Henkes. Britta has this book, and our family enjoyed the Minneapolis Children's Theatre's spring 2004 production of the play, by Kevin Kling. So this line is one of our "ties."

In this book that you are reading, I include many sample entries from the journals I'm writing for my children. But that doesn't make my kids nervous because they know that every entry is not only true but also shows them in the best light.

Rule #2: Renounce perfectionism.

Perfectionism is an enemy. It says, "Wait until you have time to do this properly." I fight back by reminding myself that the choice is not between doing it imperfectly now and doing it perfectly later. That's an illusion. The real choice is between doing it imperfectly now or not at all.

If you need extra ammunition, you might also tell yourself that you can remake the best bits into another book later—either on your computer or in another journal or in a scrapbook. Right now, the goal is to catch the thought on paper so it isn't lost.

Try not to think of this as a masterpiece; think of it as a work in progress—like life itself. A page in a journal is like a day in a life. You can't go back and do it over, but you'll have another opportunity to do it differently. Another day; another page. If you don't live this day now, when will you live it? You either live it or lose it. Just so, if you don't write down the thoughts in your mind now, when will you do it? Thoughts come and go. If you don't catch them on paper, they're likely to disappear. Memory preserves only a select few; paper or disks can preserve many more.

Being imperfect takes courage[7]—the courage of humility. The courage to say to yourself, *I may have a better idea later, or there may be a better way to do this, or I might do something differently next time; nonetheless, this is what I am doing now.*

---

[7] *The Courage to Be Imperfect* is a book by Paul Tillich. I'm not sure if I ever actually read any of the contents (and therefore can't recommend it), but the title has inspired me for years.

I refuse to think of journaling as a test of my creativity or my writing ability or my penmanship. It's just a fun way to communicate with my kids—like sending them care packages when they go to camp or e-mail when they are away from home or postcards when I travel. Journaling is one more way to say, "I'm thinking happy thoughts about you and want you to know it."

If you're hesitant to include something (something your child did or said, or a happy moment together) because you don't know what to say about it, simply don't elaborate or comment. Just write what your child said or did or the thought you had ("Thanks for the hug this morning as you left for school"), add the date, and you're done.

Rule #3: Keep journals within easy reach.

You might want to keep your journals in the kitchen cupboard or drawer, by the phone book, or next to your bed. The goal is to keep them as close as possible to wherever you'll be when you want to write in them.

I keep my current journals in a basket next to my favorite chair. A basket works well for me because I can easily grab the whole thing and move it. When overnight guests are coming, I take the basket up to my bedroom. On a cold winter morning, I might take it down by the woodstove. The kids know where their books are, and they know they are welcome to read (and to write in) them any time.

Because my books are handy, I can quickly jot something down before I forget it. For example, one evening Betsy needed me to sit in the car with her to help with homework for Go Driving School. She had to sit in the driver's seat and locate all the items listed on her worksheet. I was to sit shotgun and initial each item once she found it. The car was parked in the driveway, and after we finished her homework, she asked if she could drive it into the garage. Realize that she had never—ever—driven before. I said okay, then held my breath and prayed that she wouldn't crash through the far end of the garage. She sat tall, started the engine, and inched her way into the garage, stopping plenty short of the far wall. Then she shut off the engine, turned to me with a smile to burst the sun and said, "Mommy, we're home!"

On my way to the coat closet, I paused to scribble in her book those three words she had just said, the date, and this explanation: "—Betsy after driving the car for the first time ever from the driveway into the garage." It took perhaps ten seconds. Someday I may make a scrapbook page with those words and a photo of Betsy in the car and a photocopy of her permit. Then again, I may not. Good thing it's in her journal.

On Ripping Out Pages

If you take Rule #1 and Rule #2 seriously, as I do, you may find yourself ripping out pages from time to time. One day Jack (my youngest) read something new I had written and said sadly, "Why did you write something bad?" Oops. I quickly grabbed his book and ripped out the latest entry. Britta (three years his elder) saw all this and was shocked: "Don't rip it out! Jack might change his mind and decide he likes it later!" But Jack was happy to see it go: "Just let her rip it out if she wants to."

Journal or Diary?

A diary is generally a chronological account of events. Many people who keep a diary record their comings and goings each day. A journal, on the other hand, is generally a record of one's thoughts, ideas, interpretations, questions, or insights.

A diary has value historically and personally; a journal has value spiritually, morally, and intellectually. Some sort of combination, adapted to your personality and that of your child, is probably the ideal.

Scrapbook Journaling

You could think of scrapbooks as diaries or journals in pictures. If you keep a scrapbook and it is primarily a photo-diary, a record of what happened, you might consider adding journalistic elements. I can think of two ways to do this. The first is by writing a description of the experience and how you felt about it or what you understood the significance of it to be. Another way is to communicate a message or a theme or an impression using color and shape and artwork and inspiring quotations. I'd call both of these techniques "scrapbook journaling."

If you are good at keeping your scrapbooks current, then you may not want to write separate journals. But you may find it valuable to keep a small notebook handy to collect words and ideas that you can later incorporate into a page.

Chapter 3

Four Strategies for Non-Writers

If we eliminate the word "writer," if we just go back to writing as an act of listening and naming what we hear, some of the rules disappear.

—Julia Cameron[8]

You don't need to be a writer per se to keep a journal. This chapter presents four types of entries that don't require the journal-keeper to be creative or to "think something up," only to "get something down."

1. Listen for Dialogue or Monologues

As writing coach Julia Cameron suggests in the quotation at the beginning of this chapter, the way to begin is to listen. Simply jot down what your child says or what someone says about your child. On February 23, 2005, Betsy said, "I discovered life is much better when you do your homework." I record these things.

---

[8] Julia Cameron, *The Right to Write: An Invitation and Initiation into the Writing Life* (New York: Tarcher/Putnam, 1998), 8.

Here's an entry from Britta's book the second day of first grade.

> Your teacher told Daddy that when she said to the class, "Horses wouldn't be purple, would they?" you said, "They would if you dyed them."

Sometimes you may need to add a simple explanation so that the quote makes sense.

Jack's book 1/22/02 [He was eight]:

> "I've almost won the battle, Mom!" calls Jack from the kitchen.
> Translation: I've almost finished loading the dishwasher.

Another day—when it was Jack's job to unload the clean dishes, I recorded this little dialogue between us:

> "Mom, is the dishwasher dirty or clean?"
> "Dirty."
> "Good. I hope it stays dirty forever."

I also like to record things other people say about my children. The other day a friend called to ask if Betsy could baby sit. After I hung up the phone, I went straight to Betsy's journal to record what she said:

> 5/5/05. Julie called and asked me to tell you that she'd like you to babysit on the twenty first. Then she said, "I just have to tell you how much I appreciate Betsy as a babysitter. I really feel I can trust her with Madeline [the baby], so that's why I always call."

Betsy, that says so much about you! George MacDonald said, "It is a greater compliment to be trusted than to be loved."

By the way, you are also loved! ☺

2. Record Events

Think of your pen as a camera and simply transfer a moment or a happening onto the paper. Don't feel you have to add fancy adjectives or elaborate descriptions. You don't even need complete sentences. Just put on paper what happened so you can remember. This entry I made in both Jack's and Britta's books.

3/20/97. Spring Equinox. Britta and Jack have cranked up the *Seasons* CD, Vivaldi—It's now playing "Spring"—and they are playing along on their recorders!

Here's one from Betsy's book written when she was ten:

We've had more time to read the last few days, with your being home sick. And you've just discovered the joy of tea. You like orange herbal tea or Constant Comment with a dash of milk. We sit at the kitchen table taking turns reading aloud.

3. Make a List

One great feature of lists is that they are quick and easy. Write things down in whatever order they pop into your mind. Here are some possible subjects:

- Likes (favorite foods, favorite videos this year)
- Dislikes

- Current friends
- Skills
- Accomplishments
- Typical way of dressing this month
- Little phrases that keep popping up in conversation this week
- New words
- Questions your child has asked that you can't answer
- Prayer requests and answers to those prayers
- Verses your child has memorized
- Qualities that make your child unique
- "10 things I hope for you"
- "Adventures I'd like to take with you"
- "Books I'd love to read and discuss with you"
- "Movies that would be fun to watch together"
- "Things I always want to remember about the way you are right now"
- "Things I hope you'll remember about me"

4. Collect Things of Value

Add texture to your journal by importing treasures. You might want to have a special section of the journal for a certain category of entries; for example, in my first journals, I started putting photographs in the back. I included only photos of the two of us together—so the very back page has a snapshot of me holding my child as a tiny baby, then as you flip backward, you see the child growing older (I, of course, remain ageless).

These days, I just paste in photos in chronological order, right after whatever I last wrote. And I include a wider variety of pictures. There are many other possibilities:

- Tape in notes or cards from your child to you. This is one way to preserve your child's handwriting at various ages. In Jack's book, I taped in a page ripped from a small spiral notebook on which he had written a note and posted it by my coffee maker. Printed in nine-year-old style letters with a black marker, it says, "Please Make Sinniman rolls for Break Fast!!. Love you. Jonathan Finck." Even spelling errors are precious memories of a child's unique journey growing up. In Jack's journal I also have a card that I found waiting for me when I came home from a weekend away. It says:

Dear Mom,
    I hope you had a good time. I've been feeling lonely because we never had time for late night reads. I went to Thunder Blades with Josiah, but I lost my wallet and their was the big $5 [here a drawing of a $5 bill] in there so Dad paid me back and my room is preaty messy because I was looking for my wallot today. I'm feeling sad. [here a drawing of a sad face]. Love, Jonathan Finck
P. S. It felt like you where gone for ten years!

Every once in a while, Jack will write directly in the journal. I think it is where he goes to find me when I'm not home. I dated this one (6/4/04) when I noticed it:

Dear Mom,
    Today I am waiting for you as I write this. I'm bored and Britta was annoying me earlier today. I wish you where here. A couple of minutes ago I was reading *The Magician's Nephew* by C. S. Lewis. I just can't wait till you get home. Love, Jack.

• Incorporate your child's drawings (and yours if you are so inclined). When Britta noticed that Jack was writing in his journal, she asked if she could draw a picture in hers. I was delighted. She drew a picture of the two of us holding hands.

- Copy favorite Bible verses or quotations.
- Copy lines (even paragraphs) from books or movies, lyrics from a song your child loves. Here's a simple entry from Jack's book—a quotation I copied one evening after reading a chapter from one of *The Chronicles of Narnia* by C. S. Lewis. I love this series of books because they inspire and encourage me as much as they do my kids.

From *The Silver Chair:* The prince says to Jill and Eustace and Puddleglum, after they've killed the witch and now must venture to escape through unknown dangers, "We shall all kneel and kiss [Aslan's] likeness, and then all shake hands with one another, as true friends that may shortly be parted. And then, let us descend into the city and take the adventure that is sent us."

Here is a quotation I copied into Britta's book. I wrote a little introduction, but you wouldn't have to do that if you didn't want to.

3/20/05. We just finished the last chapter of *The Princess and the Goblins* by George MacDonald (for the second time!). It's delightful to share good books with you, Britta. We like the same parts. Whenever you say, "Underline that!" I am already reaching for a pencil.

Here is one we liked: "The king, who was the wisest man in the kingdom, knew well that there was a time when things must be done, and questions left till afterwards."

And here's another: "If a true princess has done wrong, she is always uneasy until she has had an opportunity of throwing the wrongness away from her by saying, 'I did it; and I wish I had not; and I am sorry for having done it.'"

Reading good books to our children is one of the best ways to strengthen their capacity to imagine goodness, which helps them to make good choices when they find themselves in similar circumstances. Copying key sections from a book into your child's journal will bring the whole book back to mind and not only provide a happy memory of time spent together but also reinforce the lesson.

- Paste in "scraps"—ticket stubs, museum pamphlets, bits of e-mails or magazine articles. On one page of Jack's book I taped an empty foil packet of Perfect Peach Bigelow tea. Under it I wrote: "Your favorite tea (lightly brewed, not too hot, with milk and sugar)."

Anything that will bring back happy memories of your life with your child is worth collecting.

Chapter 4

Six Strategies for Writers

We writers are lucky. Nothing bad ever happens to us.
It's all material.

—Philip Roth

Before You Decide to Skip this Chapter

You may think you don't like to write, but perhaps you haven't given it a fair chance. As William Zinsser says, "Writing is thinking on paper."[9] That's all. One of the reasons some people (I among them) enjoy writing is that it helps us figure out what we are thinking.

To get started, you just have to tell your mind to listen to what it is thinking. You might want to start with a personal journal that no one else will ever read. This gives you freedom to practice connecting your mind to the pen in your hand, letting the thoughts flow into words on the page. As you write, you may change your mind and decide to think differently. If I place myself, like a pencil, in God's hands, He can actually use my writing to "transform my mind" (Romans 12:2).

---

[9] William Zinsser makes this statement in at least two of his excellent books: *Writing to Learn* and *On Writing Well.*

Practicing—by writing a rough draft in your personal journal or on scratch paper—is a smart strategy when you are writing something a bit touchy or very important in your child's journal. It gives you a chance to try putting your thoughts into different words to discover which ones best express the idea you have in mind. I'm not talking about perfectionism. I'm just saying that writing a rough draft sometimes helps me figure out what I really want to say. I use this strategy when I want to be sure my thoughts came through with the right tone.

In Chapter 16, I discuss the Rewards of Writing for you, the writer.

Make the Form Your Own

If you enjoy using words to express your ideas, there are unlimited ways to shape your entries. Here are six suggestions to get you started.

1. Write Notes of Affection

No special occasion needed. No poetic words required. What we need is a sharp awareness of how blessed we are to have our children. One day I happened to be near Jack's school at the end of the school day, so I decided to surprise him and pick him up. But I was a minute too late. Kids were already rushing out to the transfer buses. I stood and watched for him, but he must have been among the first ones out, and I had no idea which transfer bus he rode, so I got back in my car to leave. In my spirit I felt an emptiness. I had looked for my boy and not found him. Suddenly I thought of Heather—a woman in our town whose face I had seen on the news just after a house fire killed both her sons. In fact, I had just driven by the blackened shell of her house on my way to the school a few minutes earlier. It now occurred to me that every day at this time she must ache to think that her boys are never coming home from school, never coming home from anywhere.

I cannot know how long I'll have my children. They are short-term guests in my home—to be cherished and enjoyed. So one day shortly after that experience, I scribbled this in Jack's book:

> Hi, Jack. It's Monday afternoon and I'm just thinking how much I'm looking forward to picking you up after school. The house is so quiet. I'm glad it will soon be full of your bright energy.

Here's an entry from Britta's book, written when she was a kindergartener:

> I just watched you run off to catch the school bus, and my heart was so full of delight that tears came to my eyes. I love your bright, bouncy step and the purple rose on top of your felt hat.

2. Describe a Moment

Here's the very first entry in Jack's second journal. He and I went to a bookstore together so he could pick out a new "Me & You" book. He chose one with a leather cover and a ribbon bookmark, and he wanted me to start writing in it right away while we had treats at the cafe inside the bookstore.

SHOPPING BUDDIES

August 15, 2003. forty six days till Jack's tenth birthday.

We found this handsome journal at the Barnes & Noble in Galleria Mall in Edina—after shopping for back-to-school clothes at Southdale. We left Daddy with Britta and Betsy at Limited Too and went to GAP

KIDS, where you found a reversible jacket (navy-red), blue slip-on shoes, jeans, and khakis (with Teflon coating!). You are so easy to shop with: decisive, reasonable, not covetous, careful not to spend too much of other people's (like your parents') money. And you look good in everything ☺. Now here we are in Barnes & Noble. You are reading *Two Towers* (after finishing your apple fritter). I'll take notes from some good books I found. Such pleasant company you are!

We can help our kids understand biblical principles by describing real-life moments that illustrate them. Here's an example:

3/23/04. Dear Betsy,

Last night, while you were practicing piano, Britta went into the music room to play guitar in a fit of defiance against homework and kitchen duties. She wasn't mad at you, but she seemed to be taking out her anger on you by strumming the guitar as loudly as she could from the couch right behind you—pitting her music against yours.

I heard this from upstairs and fell to my knees, asking God to melt the tension and to give you both grace. I sensed that an ugly conflict might ensue. My prayer for you was that your concentration would be magnified, intensified, unshakable—that you would be so caught up in your music that you would hardly notice the irritation/distraction. Jack noticed the music battle, too, and pointed it out to me. I asked him to pray as well. Apparently God answered our prayers. You kept right on practicing piano without a word to Britta, until she eventually strummed out all of her frustration, set down the guitar, and left the room.

You are a Romans 12:21 girl. You don't let irritations get the best of you; you get the best of them by doing good!

This entry shows Betsy two good ways to avoid conflicts: 1) prayer, and 2) focusing on doing what you're supposed to do and ignoring people who are irritating you. And the power of this lesson is that she herself was the positive role model. All I did was to take what she unintentionally did right and bring it to her attention so that in the future she can do it intentionally.

3. Keep a Correspondence

Because we live in the same house as our children, it makes sense to simply talk to them, as opposed to writing letters—unless your children are at camp or you are traveling without them. But there are times when communication can be enhanced by writing to each other. One way to do this would be to pass the journal back and forth. When Britta was in seventh grade she and a friend had a friendship journal they would pass back and forth between classes at school. Middle-school girls love this sort of thing. Certain types of kids would enjoy it at any age. You could use separate cards and letters instead of a journal, then collect them all in a box. Or you could attach letters to the journal.

I remember reading a magazine article written by a mother who shared how precious it was to carry on a correspondence with her daughter. It had started with a note from the girl to the tooth fairy, left under her pillow. The tooth fairy wrote back, and things developed from there. The correspondence added a whole extra layer of depth to their relationship and helped them communicate, especially through the girl's awkward years of adolescence. At the time the article was written, the girl was away at college; the mom was feeling gratitude for the friendship they had cultivated and enjoying the continuing letters.

4. Share Things You Are Learning

Malcolm Muggeridge once said, "Everything happening, great or small, is a parable whereby God speaks to us. The art of living is to get the message." Perhaps the most effective way to help children develop this art is to model it. When you learn something that would make sense or be of particular interest to them—especially if the occasion for your insight involved them—include it in their book.

> 1/9/99. Betsy's first basketball game.
> How beautiful you look out on the court—so tall and agile. You're a good athlete. I like how your ponytail snaps back and forth when you run and how your tongue pushes out your cheek when you really get serious.
> I learned something very interesting about life from a comment Dad made during the game: "When you don't have the ball, it's time to get yourself into position. You can make as much progress for your team without the ball in your hand as you can with it." Strategy. Setting yourself up. Very important—even in living a day well.

5. Highlight Positive Qualities

One of my favorite ways to do an entry is to describe something my child did, then comment on how that episode reveals a virtue. The following entry in Betsy's book is an example:

> Sunday night the Osborn family was visiting. Toward the end of the evening, the kids were getting restless and wild. There was division among the kids—little pairs or trios divided against each other. Then you saved the evening with a brilliant idea. You asked me for the Christmas cards I didn't want to save, and you taught

all the kids how to cut and fold the cards into little boxes. It was the perfect activity to engage everyone's interest. Thanks!

You're a good leader and good at crafts and creative solutions.

When I find myself smiling at something a kid does, that's my clue to make a quick note in his or her journal.

8/29/99. I'm downstairs having my prayer time, and the rest of the family is asleep—except a bright, clear, happy little voice singing upstairs. I smile to think of my exuberant Britta who is so glad to be alive this morning.

When Britta was in middle school, her homeroom teacher kept a poster on her wall that inspired me every time I went in for conferences. It said:

> *Watch your thoughts, they become your words.*
> *Watch your words, they become your actions.*
> *Watch your actions, they become your habits.*
> *Watch your habits, they become your character.*
> *Watch your character, it becomes your destiny.*

When I highlight my kids' positive actions, I increase the likelihood that those are the actions that will become strengthened into habits.

Jack's book, 8/24/03. Yesterday I went out to work in the garden. It was a beautiful, cool morning. You were waiting for Dad and Betsy and Britta to get ready to go to the state fair, and you asked if you could pull weeds to earn spending money. I agreed.

But when you put on your leather gloves and picked up some tools and looked around at things, you changed your mind. "Mom, I don't want to work for money. I want to work for treasure in heaven." You entered the work with your usual enthusiasm. First you noticed a jade plant that needed to be replanted, so we did that. Then you asked if you could prune some overgrown branches, then you joined me pulling weeds. When Britta asked how much spending money you had earned, you said, "I'm not working for money. I'm working for the love of the garden."

You are rich indeed, Jack—both in eternity and here on earth—to possess this love.

6. *Encourage Spiritual Growth*

You can use the journal to follow the advice of Proverbs 22:6: "Train up a child in the way he should go"; i.e., according to his or her bent.

Charles Swindoll, in his book *Growing Wise in Family Life,* says the key to Proverbs 22:6 is to begin by getting to know your child, which takes two things: first, the desire to really learn how God uniquely shaped this child, and second, time to observe him/her, pray about him/her, think about him/her.

Swindoll's counsel is to "give your child the time it takes to find out how he or she is put together. Then, when they move out into a society that seems committed to pounding them into another shape, they'll remain true to themselves."

Journaling is a practical way to do this. Simply listen to your child and record what you hear. Watch your child and record what you see. Pray for God to give you glimpses into His idea for this unique and eternal being. Ask for guidance so you can guide.

What follows is an entry from Betsy's book written after a difficult afternoon clothes shopping at the mall. Betsy must have tried on hundred pairs of jeans, and the fact that none of them fit perfectly had her feeling irritable and down. She said, "I must have a very strange body if no pair of jeans fits me right." The idea of being a unique creation of God the Master Artist didn't have much appeal to her at the time. After we got home, she left to go to a babysitting job. I noticed she took her sketch book with her. Her hobby that month was drawing designs for redecorating her bedroom. This is what I wrote in her book while she was gone.

8/16/03. What if you were designing a room—a unique room that expressed your Betsy-ness in a way that gave you great joy—particularly because it was special—unlike any other room you had ever designed?

Then what if this room went shopping at Roomdale Mall[10] and tried on things to decorate itself, but most didn't fit because they had been made with mass-produced rooms in mind? What if this special room felt sad that it was unusual and kept trying to redecorate itself to hide its uniqueness?

Wouldn't you call out to this room and say, "BEE HAPPY!"[11] Bee the Betsy Room! Let me show you my idea of you!

Isak Dinesen writes, in *Out of Africa,* that "pride is faith in the idea God had when he made us. A proud man is conscious of the idea and aspires to realize it. He does not strive towards a happiness or a comfort which

---

[10] In Minnesota, many of our malls are "dales"—Southdale, Rosedale, Ridgedale, etc.

[11] Betsy calls all of these journals "Bee Happy Books" because her previous journal had a drawing of a bumble bee on the front and the words "Bee Happy."

may be irrelevant to God's idea of him. His success is the idea of God carried through, and he is in love with his destiny."

When Betsy got home from babysitting, she gave me a note she had written in her sketch book. It said:

Dear Mom,

I'm here babysitting @ the Schuffels. I cannot handle any more sugar, so I've stopped making my Starburst chain. Instead of designing rooms, I thought I'd write you a note, which is exactly what I'm doing! I'm happy that I can call you! You have good advice on everything—including babysitting! I enjoyed our conversation ☺. I'm also happy that you wrote in my Bee Happy book. Thoughts and moments are very precious, and are usually only given to us once. Your thoughts are so special to me because it records and shows a part of who you are while you write about me ☺. That sentence isn't meant to be conceited! You know what I mean! I feel very, very good that you've started workshops on writing these books! It's such a blessing to me that you do it and it's so creative! Imagine that God is allowing you to be the calculator to multiply that blessing to many other families. It may even save some families.

Betsy's favorite subject in school is math, hence the calculator analogy. And I like it. She is doing for me the same thing I do for her—taking a small act and seeing in it the seeds of greatness. And I think she's right—writing journals will bless your family.

Chapter 5

Questions People Ask about Keeping Journals

It is the time you have wasted for your rose that makes
your rose so important.
—Antoine de Saint Exupery

Q: What kind of journal is the best to use?

A: The best journal is the one your child would love the most. You might want to take your child with you and let him or her pick one out. I started my first journal back in 1988, before the current journaling craze, so I didn't have many choices. Betsy's first book is a small, plain black sketch book I found at an art supply store. Her current book is a beautiful lilac-colored hard-bound book with butterflies imprinted on the corner of every page. Her previous journal was bright yellow, with a big bumble bee on the front along with the words "Bee Happy." She still calls all the journals Bee Happy Books. So sometimes when Jack says something funny, for example, she'll say, "Mom, write that in his Bee Happy Book." She has even come to think of her ideal self (the one I reflect back to her in her journal) as Bee Happy Betsy—as opposed to, say, Grumpy-pants Betsy.

Spiral-bound journals are my favorite. They come in just as many beautiful colors and designs as the hardbound books, and it's simple to rip out one page without disturbing other pages. Even a simple spiral-bound notebook will work. Once you get going, you may decide to "upgrade." If so, don't worry about finishing one book before starting another. Think of it as practice in renouncing perfectionism.

Q: *What if my handwriting is atrocious?*

A: Of course computers have advantages, especially if yours is quickly accessed and always available. But remember that your handwriting has value for its own sake—because it is a part of you. Even if your handwriting isn't as beautiful as you wish it were, your children will cherish it. And if it is legible, they'll read it.

An op-ed article by Joseph H. Conner, published in a newspaper just before Mother's Day, was headlined "Gigabytes Can't Capture Mom."[12] He argues that despite the ease of using modern technology, "some memories . . . might be worth holding onto . . . the old-fashioned way.

"I look at mother's slanted script in a letter to me when I was at college," he writes. "She was telling me to do my best but not to worry if I wasn't at the top, or anywhere near the top. . . . [Over the years] her handwriting became less fluid and a bit jagged and then halting. Still it was her message in her hand. And those notes embody her continuing goodwill, as well as her physical decline. I wish I had responded to her in writing . . . so that I would have actual evidence of what was going through my mind then." In the final paragraph he admonishes readers to "hold onto a few scraps of your mother's handwriting. Those exemplars can bring back memories that can't be captured in gigabytes or be erased in error. There is no time like the present to begin saving the connections to a past—a personal Intranet."

---

[12] *Christian Science Monitor,* May 7, 2004, 9.

Q: *Where do you keep completed books?*

A: In a safe place.

You've probably been asked (at some party or group function as an ice-breaker) this question: If your house were on fire and all the people and pets were safe, what would be the next thing you would grab?

How do you answer? I always say, "My journals and scrapbooks, because those are the things that are absolutely irreplaceable."

One day it occurred to me that if my house actually were on fire, I wouldn't have time to hunt through the house to find those books that I value so much. So I decided to gather them together and put them in baskets relatively near the front door. Everyone in the family knows that these are the things to save (after all the people, naturally, and then Sunni the yellow lab and Curious George the cat and Buddy the other cat and Chili the chinchilla—and of course the goldfish, whose names I can never remember).

Q: *How often do you write?*

A: As often as I can, but not often enough. The first book (that little black sketch book I kept for Betsy, which is three" wide, four" tall, and one" deep) took me ten years to fill. And the last dozen or so pages are photos (in that book, I started in the back pasting in photos of the two of us). I wish now that I had written more often. But I have to remind myself that anything is better than nothing. Betsy and I are both grateful for the memories and thoughts we do have from those years.

I certainly don't write every day. Weekly is more like it—but I don't write in each book every week. When I have something to say, I do everything reasonable to get it down as soon as possible. Some ideas get lost. Sometimes I scribble a quick note in the catch-all notebook I keep in my bag. Sometimes I make a reminder to myself on a scratch paper or Post-it note. Then I make it a high priority to sit down and write as soon as my head is clear and no urgent tasks are pressing me. Usually that means first thing the next morning—early, before anyone else in the house is awake.

Q: How do you remind yourself to write?

A: I keep my journals in sight so I don't forget them.

Also, now my children are involved enough to know when I write. They sometimes remind me when it has been too long.

Q: What if I don't want to take on such a big project?

A: You could do a modified version. Some parents have journals for each child and write in them annually, on that child's birthday, say, or at Christmas. They write an overview of the year, including the child's accomplishments and evidence of character growth.

If you don't like the idea of a book because it seems overwhelming to think about filling it, you could write letters or cards to your child from time to time and save these in a box. Chapter 4 includes a section on corresponding with your child.

A friend of mine shared with me that her father used to give her books as gifts, and he would write inscriptions on the front page. For example, in *Pilgrims Progress* he wrote, "To my Constant Joy [her name is Connie, short for Constance], May you ever be a Valiant, Faithful Pilgrim." After her father's death, these words remain alive for her—a living inspiration and a forever-bond with her father. Here's the amazing thing: Connie *is* a valiant and faithful pilgrim. I wonder how much of that is the fruit of her father having taken the time to invest in her life and to point her in the right direction—in writing.

Q: *How do you find time to write?*

A: I make time by letting go of things that are less meaningful for me. In Chapter 8, I address this challenge in more detail, but the truth is that making an entry doesn't need to take much time.

Q: *What about keeping one journal for all your children?*

A: This is a good idea, unless there might be controversy about who will inherit it after you die. Of course if you do it on a computer, you will be able to print out multiple copies. A friend of mine is writing a book for her family—the story of their life together, starting with "When Mom met Dad."

Q: *What if my children are already grown?*

A: It's never too late to say "I love you" with a journal. You can write your memories—in whatever order they occur to you. You can write new thoughts you want to share with your adult children. You can reflect for them who they are now—things they do or say that bring you joy.

Q: *What if there is already a wall between my child and me?*

A: The journal is one way to begin tearing it down. You may think your child won't want to read it, but who can resist being curious about what someone else thinks of us—especially when it is good?

Even if he or she doesn't want to read the journal now, the fact that you write it anyway is one way to demonstrate your faith in a future reconciliation. You could write your prayers and hopes for your child (always being careful that nothing could be construed as a lecture or scolding). You could write your own thoughts and ideas about subjects that interest you—things you would have chatted about if the relationship weren't strained.

Q: *Won't my child get an inflated ego if I only write positive things?*

A: One way to protect against egotism and encourage gratitude is to record in the journal the many other people who deserve credit for good aspects of your child's life; for example, the generosity of grandparents, the wisdom of teachers, the persistence of coaches, the encouragement of friends.

At the same time, don't be afraid to document good things your child does. I'm not thinking only of displays of skill. I'm also thinking of acts of kindness or courage, times when your child shows a beautiful humility or a willingness to sacrifice for the sake of others. But talents and accomplishments should indeed be recorded. If you only write true things, your child's ego won't be falsely inflated. Part of your role is to help your child figure out what unique contribution he or she can make to the greater good of the world. In order to know this, your child needs to know his or her strengths and potential.

I'm not saying that we should give children the false impression that they can do no wrong. "Love . . . keeps no record of wrongs,"[13] but it may do very well to keep a record of wrongs righted, mistakes fixed, stumbles recovered from, and lessons learned.

Our responsibility as parents includes correcting our children when they need it. But the child's mistake does not need to be documented. Children can learn from their mistakes and then forget them.

Consider this analogy. I happen to be a bad speller. When I realize I've misspelled a word, I delete the error and replace

---

[13] 1 Corinthians 13:5b NIV.

it with the proper spelling. What value would there be in saving my misspelled words? They would only confuse me and get in the way of spelling correctly in the future. My best hope for becoming a good speller is to forget, as quickly as possible, every misspelling I've ever written and to focus on the correct spelling that I have now learned. As I imprint more and more correctly spelled words into my mind, I transform myself into a good speller. Collecting all my mistakes would reinforce my idea of myself as a bad speller. Soon I'd completely give up hope of ever overcoming the problem. On the other hand, recording the words I've successfully learned to spell could reinforce lessons learned and inspire me to keep learning.

Q: Wouldn't there be value in documenting certain problems your child experiences as data to draw from as an adult?

A: I can see the value of this. As adults, we want to know how our personalities developed during childhood. Data would be helpful, especially if it gives us clues to our nature or to the events that shaped us. An accurate record of life events, both positive and negative, and a record of one's responses and reactions, both positive and negative, may be useful.

Shame is the thing to avoid.

If you think a certain bit of information may be important to record, yet your child might be ashamed to have it in the journal, you could record it elsewhere, perhaps in your personal journal, and share it with your child at an appropriate future time.

Q: Isn't it better to spend quality time with my children than to be away from them writing?

A: Yes, time spent with someone is better than time spent writing to or about that person—if it comes down to a choice.

But after you spend time with someone, it may be appropriate (even helpful) to "get away" and do some writing. Distance allows you to see some good things you might otherwise have been too close to notice.

Q: *What if I can't think of anything to write?*

A: Chapters 3 and 4 suggest ten different types of entries to get your mental wheels spinning. Once you get started, you'll think of other ideas that suit you and the person you are writing for. You could start by going shopping together for the journal. Then the first entry could be a description of that outing.

Q: *What if I have more to write to one child than I do to another?*

A: The best thing to do is to take some time to reflect on this situation. What might be the reasons for this? You may learn something about this child or yourself or your parenting style that you didn't know before. The insight may take courage to accept, but it may be the most valuable thing that comes of your doing this project. It is a gift to be received.

If you conclude that there are very few ties binding you to this child, go out of your way to establish some.

- Arrange a special date with this child, then record it in your journal.
- Let your child choose a novel—or storybook, for younger children—that just the two of you will read together. Copy some lines from that book into your journal.
- Invite only this child to accompany you on an errand or help you with one of your chores. Have someone take a snapshot of the two of you working together. In the journal, thank your child for keeping you company or helping with your chore—even if he did it grudgingly.

- Plan to spend extra time tucking this child in tonight. Give her plenty of individual attention: sing songs, rub her back, listen if she is willing to share what is on her heart. If the other children want equal time and you can't afford it tonight, then give the next child a special tuck-in tomorrow evening, and the following child the following night, and so on. In your child's journal, write the lyrics for the song you sang or make a note of what you talked about. Tell her you enjoyed spending time with her at the end of the day.

Chapter 6

Getting Started: Prompts for Parents

There is, in every child, at every moment, a miracle unfolding.
—Erik Erikson, psychologist

As a parent you have closer and more immediate access to your child than anyone else in the world. You also have the advantage of knowing your child's history and ancestry. Your observations are primary data that will be incredibly valuable to your children as they grow and struggle to understand themselves.

How to Know When It's Time to Write

When you hear yourself telling your spouse or a friend about something interesting your child said, that's your cue. Make a mental note to write that story or comment in your child's journal as soon as you can get to it.

When your child makes you chuckle in that delightful sort of way, make a note of whatever sparked that laugh. Scribble it on a scrap of paper and carry it around with you until you can tape that scrap in the journal or sit down and write an entry.

When your child speaks with the voice of an angel and tells you (perhaps without any awareness) exactly what you need to hear at exactly the right moment, stop and write a note of thanks.

The One-Liner

An entry doesn't need to be an entire page long or even a paragraph. Sometimes all you need to write is a sentence or a phrase; something like, "Today you said, '. . .'" or, "When such-and-such happened, you responded by saying [or doing]. . . ."

What you are doing is taking notes, making observations. Like a scientist trying to learn about a new species or an anthropologist studying a newly discovered people group, you study your child to discover all you can about this strange and wonderful human being that is "unique in all the world."[14] You probably know your child better than anyone else knows this child, yet every day he grows and changes and becomes slightly different because of new experiences, new discoveries, new thoughts and decisions. These are small things that can be noted in a few words. And it is well worth spending the few minutes required to make these small investments.

Another benefit of making small entries regularly is that it keeps you in the habit of journaling. This makes it easier to sit down for ten or fifteen minutes when you want to write a longer entry.

The Annual Entry

If making small entries throughout the year doesn't sound workable for you, consider writing a page or two once a year.

---

[14] One of the Little Prince's discoveries (in *The Little Prince* by Antoine de Saint Exupery) was that the rose he loved was "unique in all the world" despite the fact that a million other roses existed. This charming book is great for reading aloud to children.

My friends Mark and Cindy Wolbert have four children. Cindy is a stay-at-home mom and journals for all four kids throughout the year. Mark makes an entry for each child at least once a year, typically on that child's birthday. Here's an example from Mark:

> 8/4/03. Alicia, I cannot believe that you are five already. It has been so fun to watch you develop into a little lady. You are so pretty. You always dress so sharp and you love to fix your own hair, and you do a wonderful job of it. You are so loving and compassionate. You are so generous with your hugs and kisses. The past few days I have been sick, and you have been so sweet to me. You brought me food, kept a pillow behind my head, asked me how I was doing, and showered me with hugs and kisses.
>
> You are growing up so fast. One of the fun things that you started to do this summer is to ride the four-wheeler by yourself.
>
> It has been a huge blessing watching how you treat your cousins and friends. You love to play with Lydia. You spent a lot of time with her at the lake. She loves to play with you. And you are a great friend to Hannah Bengtson. God has given you the ability to love and encourage others.
>
> You are such a happy girl. I am so glad that you are home for one more year before you go to school. I love having you visit out at the shop and having lunch with you. Happy fifth birthday, Alicia. I love you and I am very proud of you. Love, Dad.

Any little girl would feel like a princess after reading such a love letter from her daddy. This entry includes not only words of affection but also specific details from the year—the names of her special friends, her accomplishment on the four-wheeler, her acts of kindness when Dad was sick, the facts that she would visit him in the shop and that he would come home for lunch—so it also serves to document happy moments.

They're Never Too Young

Don't wait until your child is old enough to read to begin writing love letters. Don't even wait until he is old enough to understand what is read to him. Some of your most precious memories will be from the first years, so capture them on paper now and savor them yourself. Soon enough your child will be able to enjoy them as well.

One suggestion offered by the mother of a preschooler was to print entries (as opposed to writing in script) so kids can read them sooner.

They're Never Too Old

One woman I know has started a journal for her grown daughter whose divorce is pending and who feels worthless. What better gift could you give your grown child in crisis than clear evidence that he or she is loved and cherished? Your son or daughter may not be in crisis but may still be suffering from the wear and tear of ordinary life. Words of affirmation and affection from you are like healing salve. Remember that a common affliction of adults is the haunting belief that they were never good enough to win their parents' love and approval. While you may think your son or daughter doesn't suffer from that disease, wouldn't it be better to make absolutely sure?

You may have been so busy when your children were young that you didn't have much time to stop and savor the life you shared. It's not too late. Sit down with a journal and record memories as they come to you. No need to worry about keeping things chronologically correct. You might start an entry something like this: "I'm just sitting here thinking about what you were like when you were seven . . ." or "Today something reminded me of the time when you . . ."

They're Never Too Tough

April Austin shared with me that her typical tough-guy nine-year-old son read an entry she wrote about him and said, "When you say such nice things to me it's like flowers and diamonds coming out of your mouth." All people, because of our human nature, have a need for love and encouragement. Parents can help children learn how to give and receive warmth by giving and receiving it themselves. Journal entries can document both your love for your child and your delight in your child's expressions of love to you. My son is now twelve, and every week I see him becoming more aware of what's cool and what's not (which makes me cringe). He's very tuned in to his friends and to sports. Yet for Christmas last year he gave me a page of scrapbooking stickers that were phrases like "What I love about you" and "There's just something about you." The card said, "Dear Mom, This is for the 'Me and You' book! Love, Jack."

They're Never Too Teenaged

While teenagers are trying to establish their identity as individuals, it may be hard to find connecting points or things you honestly admire about them. All the more reason to try. Keeping a journal reminds you that you need to keep finding positive things to write.

Start by making a gentle effort to enter your teenager's world. You might try offering to help her with her homework, only to realize that you have no clue how to do whatever they're doing in algebra. Then you can write an entry about how amazed you are that she can actually do those difficult problems.

If your teen is involved in music or sports or drama or speech or chess or any other program, attend the performance and write an entry about how well he did. If you have a camera, take a snapshot and include it. I know one eighth grader who tells her parents not to come to her tennis matches because she gets too nervous, but I don't believe her. I think it would be better for her parents to say they are so proud of her that they can't stay away. She would soon get used to having them there and be grateful for the support and affirmation. The wonderful thing about being a parent in these situations is that you can leave all the criticism to the coaches and simply be your teenager's No. 1 fan.

Watching videos together might be a way for you to connect with your teen, if you can find one you both want to see. The Web site www.screenit.com provides useful and detailed information that can help you avoid movies with harmful elements and find those with redeeming qualities. If your son or daughter finds a movie that looks harmless and wants to watch it with you, jump at the chance, even if it's not a movie you would normally watch on your own, or maybe one you've already watched several times.

Last Saturday night it was seventeen degrees below zero here in Minnesota (it's January). My daughter had a friend over. They were going to watch *Dead Poets' Society* and asked if I wanted to watch it with them. I did have something else I had planned to do that evening, but I decided to take them up on the offer. For one thing, the television is in the same room as the woodstove, which makes it the warmest and coziest room of the house; for another, I thought it would be nice to spend time with them. And, of course, I do like this movie. During the scene where Knox Overstreet gets up his courage to call the girl of his dreams, Betsy said, "He's my favorite character." After the movie, I asked her what she liked about him. She said, "He's so romantic." Later I wrote this in her journal:

1/17/05. Saturday night we watched *Dead Poets' Society*. Your favorite character is Knox Overstreet because he's so romantic. He's in love with Chris, a girl who is "practically engaged" to a handsome bully who goes to her school. You love the way Knox takes risks to woo her. Even after her boyfriend beats him up, Knox sneaks into her school, brings her flowers, and reads her the poem he wrote. Such a strong, undaunted love is beautiful, and Chris finally recognizes that.

Betsy, God has that kind of love for you. He woos you with beautiful sunsets, with daylilies on summer mornings, with His Word, and with music He puts in your soul for you to discover. It is a strong, undaunted love. And you are rich because you welcome it, receive it, enjoy it, and return it.

In the journal I said more than I did in the conversation we had during and after the movie because conversations jump quickly from one topic to the next. We don't always have time to think an idea through and then express it fully. Moreover, teenagers aren't always in the mood to discuss profound ideas. But they are flattered when we take little things they say and develop them into deeper concepts. It shows that we really listen to them, and it shows that their insights are the seeds of significant ideas.

If you like the idea of using movies as springboards for discussions or journal entries, you might like a book like *Movie Nights: 25 Movies to Spark Spiritual Discussions with Your Teen*.[15] A few of the movies covered are *The Count of Monte Cristo, The Truman Show, The Princess Bride, Groundhog Day,* and *Life is Beautiful*.

---

[15] Bob Smithouser, ed., *Movie Nights: 25 Movies to Spark Spiritual Discussions with Your Teen* (Wheaton, Illinois: Tyndale, 2002).

Other Ideas for Entries

- After your child's birthday, tape the card from you into the journal.

- On New Year's Eve, you could spend some time with each child, talking through the previous year and listing highlights in your journal. Or you could make this a family activity and part of your New Year's Eve celebration. Go through the family calendar together, reminiscing about the year in chronological order. Kids who are old enough can list the events they want to remember in their own journals. You might want to include visits from friends and relatives, major weather events such as blizzards or hurricanes, movies you watched together, big sports games or concerts, and local and world events that will help put his or her life in perspective years from now.

- On New Year's Day, talk about the idea of resolutions with your kids. Let them each decide on a resolution or two, then you might make resolutions as a family. This year our family resolved to plan two family nights a month. Our second resolution was to read more. My husband and I each resolved to read at least one book aloud to each of the three kids and one to each other. Sharing books is one of the strongest ways to weave a common family culture. (For book ideas, see the Appendix.) You can record the resolutions in your child's journal. Older children might prefer to make this entry themselves.

- If you need to travel without your child, and if you happen to pass a shop that sells cards, buy a card that you think your child will like. On it, you might tell your child why and how much you miss him. Or describe something you saw that reminded you of him or why the card made you think of him. You can mail the card even if you'll be home before it arrives (or tuck it into your suitcase to hand deliver upon your return). After he has opened it, ask him if he wants you to tape it in his journal.

- What inspires your child? Note it in her journal. As people age, we typically experience seasons in life that are dry and without inspiration. It's good to remember things that inspired us at earlier times.
- When do you notice your daughter truly enjoying herself?
- What piques your son's curiosity?
- Write an entry about a certain character quality that your child has and list examples of times you saw him exhibiting that quality.
- Record samples of daily life at home. Pick one day and list every detail from the moment your child wakes up to the moment she falls asleep. Twenty (or forty) years from now, all these ordinary details will be a little time capsule. You and your adult child can read it together and have a nostalgic moment.

Chapter 7

Getting Started: Prompts for Grandparents

There's an upside to grandparenthood.
You play, you give, you love, then you hand them back
and go to an early movie.

—Billy Crystal

"My grandmother made all the difference in my life," a friend told me recently. I've heard similar comments from other people. Sometimes a grandparent is the only one who has time to really listen to a child or to spend hours doing those non-urgent things a parent simply doesn't have time to do. Sometimes when children feel misunderstood by parents, they need a grandparent to comfort them, encourage them, believe in them.

"The most essential role of grandparents," says Stephen Covey,[16] is to communicate, in as many ways as possible, the worth and potential of their children, grandchildren and great grandchildren so clearly that they really believe it and act on that belief. If this spirit suffused our culture and society, the impact

---

[16] Stephen R. Covey, *The 8th Habit: From Effectiveness to Greatness.*

on the civilization of the world would be unimaginably magnificent." Children are looking for someone to help them figure out who they are and who they can be. This may sound like an overwhelming responsibility, but it isn't. It simply means being there, paying attention to everything about your grandchildren that is good or beautiful or true, and actively noticing it.

You probably do this naturally—as an expression of your love. I want to encourage you to make the extra little effort to put your reflections on paper. You can keep a journal/notebook and make entries from time to time. Or you could send your grandchild letters or cards. Or jot down your memories and thoughts on whatever paper is available and collect those sheets in a box, drawer, or three-ring binder.

Here are some ideas to get you started.

Ideas for Entries

- Write your grandchild an affectionate note letting her know that you've noticed one of her good qualities. Here's a journal entry that one grandmother shared with me:

> Dear Haley, I love the way you notice the things around you that are beautiful and harmonious! I've also seen that you enjoy creating beautiful things. Thank you for all the wonderful pictures you have drawn for Grandpa and me over the years. Love, Grandma

The woman who wrote this told me that Haley is five years old and is the middle child between a very bright older brother who demands attention and a "special needs" younger sister who requires extraordinary amounts of both time and attention. Mom and Dad have all they can do to keep up with their two high-maintenance children, so who has time for Haley? Grandma to the rescue! Grandma is the one who knows how to make Haley feel like she's the most important person in the world—because Grandma is making a book about Haley!

- Write about a happy memory you have of your grandchild.

Here's an entry that Ruth Ann Kragt shared with me.

Dear Bethany,
   You truly are a joy. It's so nice to have you live right next door. I can watch you grow into a very beautiful young lady inside and out. I really miss our little shopping trips to St. Cloud. You told me on one of them that you wouldn't have any jeans if I didn't take you shopping. Now you can take yourself in your own "truck."
   I also love to watch you ride across the field at a full gallop on Jumbo, your horse. I remember when you were afraid of your first horse, Whisper. How you have grown! I'll love you forever and always. Love, Grandma

- Write a chatty letter to your grandchild, telling about the details of your thoughts and your life right now, today, this afternoon. Julia Cameron says that it was through letters from her grandmother that she learned the value of taking her mind off herself and her troubles and paying attention to the beautiful and interesting things happening around us.

   My grandmother was gone before I learned the lesson her letters were teaching: Survival lies in sanity, and sanity lies in paying attention. Yes, her letters said, Dad's cough is getting worse, we have lost the house, there is no money and no work, but the tiger lilies are blooming, the lizard has found that spot of sun, the roses are holding despite the heat.

My grandmother knew what a painful life had taught her: Success or failure, the truth of a life has little to do with its quality. The quality of life is in proportion, always, to the capacity for delight. The capacity for delight is the gift of paying attention.[17]

Julia was too young to understand the lesson from these words while her grandmother was still alive. If the thoughts hadn't been put into words on paper, and the pages saved, that wisdom would have been lost.

- Describe what you enjoy most about your grandchild at this particular age.
- Thank your grandchild for a good time you spent together. Here's an example, written by Peggy Crooms:

    Katie,
    How I enjoyed our time in the closet! Kylie and I truly loved the great stories you told us about Barbie and Ernie and your other toys. And wasn't it fun that Grandpa couldn't find us even though we were giggling!

- Write a paragraph or make a list of things describing yourself when you were the age your grandchild is now.
- Do a comparison/contrast. You might divide the page into three columns. On the left, you can put topics or questions. In the middle, put a title like "Grandpa at

---

[17] Julia Cameron, *The Artist's Way: A Spiritual Path to Higher Creativity,* (New York: G. P. Putnam's Sons, 1992), 52.

age ten." On the right, put something like "Shannon at age ten." Your first item might be what year it was (for you) and is (for your grandchild). Your next item might be the place you each lived. Here's an example. You can adjust the questions to fit your grandchild's age and interests.

Question	Grandpa at Age 10	Shannon at Age 10
What year is it?	1935	2006
Where do you live?		
What do you eat for breakfast?		
What is your favorite game?		
Who are your best friends?		
What do you like to wear to school?		
What books have you read recently?		
What music do you like to listen to?		
Do you play an instrument?		
Do you compete in sports?		
How far have you traveled from home?		
What's your favorite subject in school?		
What do you know how to bake or cook?		
Do you have an idea of what you want to be when you grow up?		

As a variation of this chart, you could do a comparison between your grandchild at his or her current age and your child (your grandchild's mom or dad) at that same age. You are the expert because you've seen both of them up close and personal! You can note personality traits and talents that you see in both of them. Kids love to know from whom they inherited their artistic or musical or athletic abilities as well as their idiosyncrasies.

- Jot down a funny or clever thing your grandchild said.
- Make a list of books you hope your grandchild will read. You could include a quotation from the book or a few sentences about why the book meant something to you. Sharing your thoughts about the book or how it changed you will add meaning to the book. It becomes a link to you.
- Write an account of something in your life that started as a problem but turned out to be a door to something good. This will be especially powerful if there is a connection with something your grandchild is struggling with now, but a timely link is not necessary. Once the story is in the child's journal, it is available for years to come. There may come a time when your grandchild needs your example of transforming problems into opportunities.
- What have you learned about the power of kindness?
- How did you develop courage?
- How did you learn to swim?
- What do you want to be remembered for?
- What have you let go of?
- What, in your life journey so far, did you think you could not handle, yet you did? How were you able to manage?
- When have you felt particularly loved?
- How did you meet your spouse?
- Who are the five people who most impacted your life? How are you different because of each one of them?
- Do you have a special family recipe? Include it in the journal along with an account of one time you remember the family sharing this favorite dish.

- Describe things you and your grandchild have done together.
- List adventures you hope the two of you will be able to have in the future.
- Describe a moment when you felt especially close to your grandchild.
- Tape into the journal your favorite photo of your grandchild. Describe what you like about it. See if you can find pictures of yourself and your grandchild that show the family resemblance.

An Ideal Gift

I am not a grandparent yet myself, but I've observed one trait that appears to be universal among those who have achieved that status: Grandparents love to give their grandchildren gifts.

As a parent of children who have received numerous gifts from their grandparents, I have opinions on this topic. Some gifts, I submit, are better than others. The best gifts have the following qualities.

1. They do not make noise.

Avoid fire trucks that make a screeching siren noise if you push a certain button and play a tape of a loud voice saying repeatedly, "If you need help, dial 911," when you push another button. Also avoid story books with a row of noisemakers on the side.

2. They do not clutter up the house.

Avoid anything too large to fit in the child's bedroom.

3. *They don't cramp the kid's style.*

Avoid unrequested clothes and room decorations.

4. *They are age appropriate.*

Be careful not to hand down family heirlooms or breakable treasures until a child is old enough to appreciate and care for them. When my son Jack was a little boy, his great-grandfather gave him a handsome music box. Unfortunately, it soon got bumped off Jack's dresser, and a bird's wing broke off.

5. *They are meaningful.*

My son, when he was age ten and able not only to handle but also to appreciate valuable objects, was given, by my husband's father, a real sword that once belonged to my husband's grandfather. Very cool. That gift is cherished.

6. *They are personal.*

Once when I was a little girl, one of my grandmothers sewed for me half a dozen beautiful outfits with incredible detailing: smocked dresses, a pleated skirt (like the one Eloise wears), pinafores—I felt like a princess. And here's the amazing thing: She made my Chatty Cathy doll the exact same wardrobe so we could match! Whenever I think of it, I remember feeling like the luckiest girl in the world.

7. *They stand the test of time.*

Cookies are an exception to this rule.

8. *They express your love.*

Keeping a journal for your grandchild is an ideal gift. It is noiseless, small, easy to store, adaptable to the child's age and to your personal style of journaling, meaningful, enduring, and an obvious expression of love.

I have in my home an embroidered wall hanging that used to belong to my Grandma Irma. It says, "A friend is like an angel who holds on when others let go." As a grandparent, you are in the perfect position to be that kind of friend. Keeping a special journal for each grandchild is one way to show them that you intend to hold on, even if everyone else lets them go.

Chapter 8

Secrets for Finding Time

Many things can wait. The child cannot.
Now is the time . . . his mind is being developed.
To him, we cannot say tomorrow. His name is today.
—Gabriella Mistral

I remember reading a magazine article written for young moms who were having trouble getting enough sleep. The solution went something like this: "In a multiple-choice situation where one of the options is sleep, choose sleep."

This is terrific advice because it acknowledges the painful reality that life doesn't always offer you ideal options. You have to take a realistic view of your choices and go for the best one. The way to prepare for this is to carefully think through your priorities. Then, as soon as you have discretionary time, use it for your top priority. Once that is taken care of, move on to your second priority. Writing to my children is among my top priorities, so I'll let other things go in order to do it. I don't completely give up these things; I just let them go from time to time.

Clarifying What Really Matters to You

Richard Weaver said, in 1948, "It seems to me that the world is now more than ever dominated by the gods of mass and speed and that the worship of these can lead only to the lowering of standards, the adulteration of quality, and, in general, to the loss of those things which are essential to the life of civility and culture." In the half century since he said that, nothing has slowed down.

When the messages coming at us say, "Gotta do more; gotta have more,"[18] it's hard to shut out those voices long enough to ask, "Why? Exactly what am I doing with my life, and is that what truly matters to me? What do I really want? What is the highest use of the precious hours and days I've been given?"

If you take time to seriously answer those questions, you'll get a sense of your priorities. Journaling will obviously not be at the very top of your list, but I suspect that it won't be at the bottom, either. You might want to take a minute right now to list all the things that are truly more important to you than journaling for your child. This list might include things like

- Getting enough sleep to function effectively
- Making sure everyone in the family is clean, well fed, and clothed
- Keeping promises and performing required duties (going to work, for example)
- Spending time listening to and reading to my child
- "Sharpening the saw," as Stephen Covey says. This includes keeping fit physically, emotionally, socially, and spiritually. If we neglect self-maintenance, we'll soon be of no use to our families.
- Cleaning up the spilled juice on the floor

---

[18] This is a line from the movie *Dead Poets' Society.*

- Returning phone calls or e-mails from your agent or your lawyer or your mother
- Unclogging the toilet

Now think about all the things you do during the course of a week that are *not* more important than investing in your child's legacy. Make a list of things that could legitimately be postponed for ten minutes or even be moved from today's to-do list to another day. How about:

- Reading the newspaper
- Doing the dishes
- Returning non-urgent calls and e-mails
- Gardening
- Doing laundry that isn't needed tomorrow
- Dealing with piles of mail
- Personal reading

I'm not suggesting that you quit doing any of these things (or whatever things are on your non-urgent list). I'm only suggesting that from time to time you might consider postponing one to carve out time to write a love letter to your child.

In addition to the things you can postpone, there may be some things in your life that you could actually cut out if you don't find that they add to the quality of your life or anyone else's.

Leith Anderson told the following story as part of a radio address on the subject of priorities. Charles M. Schwab once asked a management consultant named Ivy Lee for a way to get more things done. "If it works," he said, "I'll pay you anything within reason." Lee suggested that he write down the things he had to do the following day, then number them in the order of their importance. First thing in the morning, he should start in on item number one and stay with it until it was done. Then move on to the second item. If he didn't get to the bottom of the list, it wouldn't matter because he would have done the things that were most important. Ivy said, "The secret is to do this daily. Evaluate the relative importance of the things you have to get done . . . establish priorities . . . record your plan of action . . . and stick to it. . . . After you have convinced yourself of the value of this system, have your associates try it. Test it as long as you like. Then send me a check for whatever you think the idea is worth." A few weeks later, Charles Schwab sent Ivy Lee a check for $25,000.[19]

Clarifying your priorities gives you freedom to move ahead and act on the highest ones, knowing that you are putting your time and energy where they matter most.

Learn a Lesson from Obsession

People who are in love have all kinds of time for their beloved. When a boy falls in love with a girl, he thinks about her all the time. If he can't be with her, he calls her. If that's impossible, he e-mails or writes her notes. Everything else in his life has to fit into the little bit of time left over.

Obviously, living in such an extreme state is impractical, but we can learn something from this and apply it to our own lives with moderation. The point is that love finds a way. When we passionately care about another person, all our creativity comes awake to help us find ways to express that love.

What If I Have More than One Child?

Rotate. This week (or this month) make your top priority to find something to write in your first child's book. Be alert to

---

[19] Leith Anderson, "Priorities: Deciding and Doing What Is Most Important. Luke 9:51–62," *Faith Matters*, www.faithmatters.fm, a broadcast ministry of Leith Anderson and Wooddale Church, 6630 Shady Oak Road, Eden Prairie, MN 55344, 952-944-6300, 1.

every positive thing she does or says, take time to listen to her, invite her to spend time with you, take pictures of her or of the two of you together. Next week (or next month), make your top priority finding something good to write to your next child. Then move on to the third for however many days it takes to think of something good to write. And so on through the sixteenth, or however many children you are blessed to call yours.

PART II

REAPING THE FRUIT

Chapter 9

The Journal as a Loving Mirror

*Be it true or false, what is said about men often has
as much influence upon their lives, and especially upon
their destinies, as what they do.*
—Victor Hugo, from *Les Miserables*

We live in a fallen, broken world. People reflect back to us ugly, harsh images of who we are to them or impossible images of who they expect us to be.

Love, on the other hand, "keeps no record of wrongs. Love does not delight in evil, but rejoices with the truth. It always protects, always trusts, always hopes, always perseveres."[20] This is the highest approach to parenting and the best reason for keeping a journal for your child.

Some parents may ask, "What about training and correction and discipline?" These are crucial aspects of parenting, but don't need to be documented in your journal unless they can be presented positively, as discussed in the "Encouraging Spiritual Growth" section of Chapter 4.

---

[20] 1 Corinthians 13: 5–7.

The Journal as Mirror

The Bible is "the perfect mirror of God's law, the law of liberty" (James 1:25 PHILLIPS). God's book to us is the perfect mirror because it shows us not only who we are—sinners in need of a Savior—but also who we were made to be—image bearers of God. As we read we find hope and freedom from bondage.

The books we keep for our children can imitate the Book that God wrote to us in a small and, of course, imperfect way. We can use our books as loving mirrors to let our children see who they are—and who they can be. This is a gift I can give to my own children in a way that no one else can. And you can give these gifts to whomever you are journaling for in a way that no one else can. Every relationship in the world is one of a kind.

One day I found Betsy's book lying open on my desk with a note on top of it that said, "WRITE . . . PLEASE, PLEASE!"[21] When I asked what I should write, she said, "Something nice about me." She reads her journal with the same intensity that she studies the mirror, trying to figure out who she is. And she checks for new entries with the same eagerness that she checks her e-mail—hoping someone was thinking about her and had something to say to her.

She likes when I unpack an ordinary moment and find in it a memory to cherish. This sort of thing:

> July 3, 2004, 6:30 p.m.
> YOU are just what the doctor ordered. I was feeling anxious, under pressure, distracted—
> You came into the kitchen, saying, "Have you read this one?" and proceeded to read me joke after joke

---

[21] "Please Please," by Alicia Aspenwall, is a short story my children used to request frequently. We found it on p. 33 of *The Children's Book of Virtues*, edited by William J. Bennett (New York: Simon and Schuster, 1995).

from the new issue of *Reader's Digest*. We laughed and laughed. I feel so much better now ☺.

Or this from May 6, 2004:

> 6:02 a.m. Just came in from the front yard, where Betsy called me to come enjoy the color of the sunrise, the spring smell (which she says is her favorite of all smells), the buds bursting everywhere, and the hole in the yard (what little animal lives there?). Julia Cameron says, "The quality of our lives is determined—always— by our capacity for delight. And the capacity for delight is the gift of paying attention." You, Betsy, have a great capacity for delight. Thanks for sharing it with me. What a lovely way to start the day!

One day she was helping chaperone the elementary kids during an activity day at church. I stopped by for something, and she came to the door to greet me. This is what I later wrote in her journal.

> When I stopped by church today, you came to the door as if you owned the place—so alive and happy, so "there"—fully real in the moment. It brought to mind a quotation from Jim Elliot:
>
> "Wherever you are, be all there. Live to the hilt every situation you believe to be the will of God."
>
> I found that quotation in a book that Jim's wife, Elisabeth, wrote to their daughter. Elisabeth says, "You have been, almost from birth, not only accepting but exuberant in your acceptance."
>
> Yes! That's my Betsy! She exuberantly accepts the gift of reality here and now. She blossoms into God's idea of her.

We learn who we are, and become who we become, in the context of relationships. Children look for nourishing relationships, for the kind of togetherness we were designed to enjoy. I want to make sure they know they can find that in me, so they don't have to go begging for it from less appropriate (and perhaps less safe) relationships. The journals show each child that I am deeply invested in our relationship and that I truly delight in being part of their lives.

Mirroring as a Vital Gift

According to psychologist Alice Miller, young children have a legitimate need for "respect, echoing, understanding, sympathy, and mirroring." The healthiest way to have this need met, she says, is through "the presence of a person who is completely aware of them and takes them seriously, who admires and follows them . . . a confidante, comforter, adviser and supporter." God's plan was for parents to fill this role, thus allowing children to develop a healthy sense of themselves as individuals. But if this need is not met in early life, the deprived children tends to go through life trying to find someone else who will love them unconditionally and pay complete attention to them. This need, which was legitimate in a young child, leads to unrealistic expectations in adult relationships.

Sometimes insecure parents, who were, perhaps, never properly loved by their own parents, expect their children to meet this need to be admired and supported and consoled, says Miller. They may tell themselves they are teaching their children to "respect" them, but what they are really doing (when the concern is for the parent's pride, not the child's character) is using the child to meet their narcissistic need to be admired and listened to and made much of.

As parents, we must be careful not to use our children to meet our own unmet needs but instead do our best to meet their needs so they can grow up healthy and secure, able to be loving parents to their own children. How can we go about doing this? The first step might be to find alternate ways to meet our own emotional needs. If we let God and good Christian friends fill our hearts, it is easier to pour out love to our children, giving them large doses of time, paying careful attention to their inner worlds, listening and showing empathy, allowing them to be themselves, guiding without shaming. A journal is helpful first of all because the process of writing requires us to be attuned to our child's emotions and experiences. Also, it shows our children that they are indeed the main character in the story of their lives (narcissistic parents treat children as minor characters or even props in the parent's personal drama). Writing the journal puts the parent in the role of coach, encourager, supporter, and mirror.

The Journal as a Tool to Understand Your Child

When we record reflections of our child's emerging personality, we help them understand themselves and at the same time help ourselves understand them. I recorded the following incident in Britta's journal when she was four. We had just returned from an appointment at the elementary school, where someone tested her to see if she was ready for kindergarten.

> 12/16/94. At preschool screening the teacher gave you a little test to see if you can repeat a whole sentence. She said, "Britta, can you say, 'I like to play in the rain?'"
> You said, "I like to play in the rain, but I would rather play in the mud."
> And that's the truth!

Compare an entry from 12/16/03—nine years later to the day. She was thirteen.

Yesterday I was waiting in the car for you—we were late for something—and as you came around to the front passenger door, you paused to make a design with your finger in the frost on the back car window.

I said, "Britta, did you forget that we're late, or are you being rude on purpose to make others wait for you?"

"Neither one," you answered. "I was enjoying life." (And you said this without a hint of defensiveness—a simple explanation.)

The earlier entry about the artistic, playful little girl helped me understand (and try to be patient with) the artistic, playful teenager. If I had scolded her for doing something wrong, she would have been confused and hurt. The truth is that there's nothing wrong with enjoying life. But this was a situation where she had to choose between two good things: having fun and being on time. And in this case, being on time was a higher good than enjoying the frost on the window. In her journal I continued:

Robert Frost said, "The woods are lovely, dark, and deep, but I have promises to keep." The joy of keeping a promise lasts longer than the joy of lingering in the woods—or in the frost. But in moments when there is no promise to keep, the highest good is to enjoy life in the moment.

Reflecting Clues to Your Child's Life Purpose

Parents are in the perfect position to notice and record crucial information about a child's development that will be tremendously helpful as children grow up and seek to understand God's plan for their lives. What piques your son's curiosity? When does your daughter really wake up and pay attention? What makes your kids laugh? When do they seem happy and expansive or peaceful and engaged? Record this information in the journal so your children can remember and reflect on it when they are making important life decisions.

By noting what your child enjoys and shows interest in, you help your child gather valuable data. Paul C. Holinger, M.D., says, "As your child develops, learning how to identify and express what she enjoys is an important step in becoming a mature adult who is able to pursue interests that provide stimulation, gratification, and a sense of accomplishment. It is not too much to say that the seeds of a successful career grow and blossom, in part, because of the way you respond to your child's earliest signals of enjoyment."[22] Dr. Holinger recommends noticing, validating, and using words to explain an infant's emotional signals—even if your child doesn't yet understand those words. A journal can hold your words until your child is able to read and understand them. Keeping a journal can increase your attunement with your children by providing a place to record happy discoveries or moments of delight.

We don't know what facts about our child's emerging personality will prove significant, and we obviously can't record everything. But if you notice some interesting propensity, you might take a minute to make a note of it. Your entry could be as simple as, "You really delight in socializing. Today when I told you we were going to visit Jenny and her mom, you squealed with glee," or, "Yesterday when we were playing at the park I noticed that you seemed happier sitting a bit back from the other kids. You seemed almost to be observing and analyzing them.

---

[22] Paul C. Holinger, M.D., *What Babies Say Before They Can Talk: The Nine Signals Infants Use to Express Their Feelings* (New York: Simon and Schuster, 2003).

I wonder what fascinating thoughts are spinning around in that tiny head of yours."

Sometimes, as I read old entries, I see the first threads of what later becomes a theme in the tapestry of my child's character. When Britta was barely four years old, I recorded that she said, "When I find all the colors, I will be a great artist." Since then I've noticed and noted many other glimpses into her artistic nature.

Jack has always loved books and information and learning. One day when I was researching something at home, he offered to help and tried to convince me that we should go to the library. "In a library," he said (and I jotted it down in his book), "you have a mountain of books around you. You can investigate anything!" Another day I recorded that he said, "It feels good to be organized."

A moment, a casual remark, a spontaneous act, a choice made with or without thought: any of these may be a window into the person your child is becoming. I try to frame a few of these comments or actions by putting them in words on paper.

When counselors try to help adults find their purpose in life, they sometimes ask, "What did you love to do when you were ten years old—just before you started trying to be who you thought everyone else wanted you to be? What were you inspired to do for the sheer joy of doing it?" The answers to these sorts of questions provide insight about who you are, your unique abilities and passions. They provide hints about God's calling on your life, your purpose, the contribution you can make in the world.

Don't you sometimes wish you could replay your life at age ten or twelve and get a glimpse into your young soul? By journaling moments from your child's life, you are giving your child that priceless gift.

The Value of an Accurate Mirror

Once our children venture out into the world, they'll hear plenty of confusing messages—particularly about who they are or who they should be. Those messages can have a crippling effect on a tender soul. Consider the damage done in this little fable:

THE MISINFORMED EAGLE

A man found an eagle's egg and put it in a nest of a barnyard hen. The eaglet hatched with the brood of chicks and grew up with them.

All his life the eagle did what the barnyard chicks did, thinking he was a barnyard chicken. He scratched the earth for worms and insects. He clucked and cackled. And he would thrash his wings and fly a few feet into the air.

Years passed and the eagle grew very old. One day he saw a magnificent bird above him in the cloudless sky. It glided in graceful majesty among the powerful wind currents, with scarcely a beat of its strong golden wings.

The old eagle looked up in awe. "Who's that?" he asked.

"That's the eagle, the king of the birds," said his neighbor. "He belongs to the sky. We belong to the earth—we're chickens." So the eagle lived and died a chicken, for that's what he thought he was.[23]

The misinformed eagle needed a clear-minded parent to tell it the truth about itself. Note that it would have to be the truth.

---

[23] Anthony de Mello tells this story in his book *The Perils and Opportunities of Reality* (Bantam Doubleday, 1990).

A loving parent would never have told the confused eagle that it was a tiger or a human being or a swan. Deception like that, especially disguised as flattery, destroys.

But your child may have unrealized potential, untapped inner resources, undeveloped talents. Perhaps this child has already left home and is out in the world surrounded by chickens who don't draw out these beautiful qualities. Perhaps your child is stuck in a barnyard, where flight seems not only impossible but irrelevant.

Here is an opportunity for practical love. Write down what you notice—all the little details that, when seen clearly, shine as evidence of "eagleness."

- Things said
- Actions taken
- Decisions made
- Responses given
- Courage shown
- Capacities revealed

This can be one of the ongoing entries that you start now and take up again later with something like, "I saw it again today—that amazing balance in your soul—your ability to bend without breaking" and fill in specific details (words, actions) as evidence.

Think for a minute about your own experience. When you were growing up, how important was your mother's opinion of you? How valuable was your father's approval and blessing? How meaningful would it be if you had in your possession even one letter from your mom detailing all the things she loved most about you? Or a card from your dad describing his vision of who God made you to be? Wouldn't it be helpful to read your parents' insights into your character and your potential? Especially if your parents were (perhaps still are) your biggest fans?

You can give your child this gift: a mirror that reflects your child in the best possible light—the light of your love.

Chapter 10

Bridges that Can Be Crossed Again and Again

> *Affection is responsible for nine-tenths of whatever solid and durable happiness there is in our natural lives.*
> —C. S. Lewis in *The Four Loves*

A word of encouragement is like a bridge that connects you to the person who said it (or the person to whom you said it).

Building a Better Bond

The circle of our personal worlds is wide. We have so many acquaintances, colleagues, relatives, and friends that it is a major challenge just to keep in contact with all the people we love and care about. Add to this all the activities and relationships our children are involved in and the connections made through them, and it's no wonder we feel pulled away from the very people who need us most.

It takes initiative, creativity, and careful planning to protect the time I have to spend with my family—and with each person in my family individually. But whatever it takes, it's worth it.

The journals help celebrate my relationship with each child by preserving my memories of the times we spend together.

When Jack was in elementary school, he always signed me up to chaperone his class field trips. After our adventures, we would paste a postcard or other souvenir in his "Me & You Book." Britta loves the collection of photos we have of the two of us. Whenever our family goes on outings, she asks someone to take a snapshot of her with me, and we tape these in her book.

Perhaps you and your child go on "dates"—just the two of you (one child likes fishing trips, another loves shopping adventures, another enjoys concerts). Or maybe you have traditional activities you do together on special occasions (decorate the house, bake the holiday treats). Maybe the two of you work together on certain routine tasks (you have a "gardening buddy" or a "laundry helper"). Each child wants to know that you really enjoy his or her company, that you are interested in getting to know what makes him or her unique. And as we spend one-on-one time together, we create the free and open space for the self-disclosure necessary for deep relationships.

Recording your dates and your ordinary moments together in your journal preserves and enhances their significance. It also proves that they actually happened. I've heard several women, whose children are now grown, say that their children have said things like, "You never spent time with me." These parents wish they had documented the many events as they happened. Remember to record non-events as well: ordinary afternoons, typical morning routines, details that will help you remember the flavor of these days after this season is over.

Establishing Ties

Let me share with you an excerpt from *The Little Prince* by Antoine de Saint Exupery. This dialogue takes place during the scene in which the little boy meets a fox for the first time and doesn't understand why the fox cannot play with him.

"I cannot play with you," the fox said. "I am not tamed. . . ."

"What does that mean—'tame'?" [asked the little prince.]

"It is an act too often neglected," said the fox. "It means to establish ties. . . . My life is very monotonous," he said. "I hunt chickens; men hunt me. All the chickens are just alike, and all the men are just alike. And, in consequence, I am a little bored. But if you tame me, it will be as if the sun came to shine on my life. I shall know the sound of a step that will be different from all the others. Other steps send me hurrying back underneath the ground. Yours will call me, like music, out of my burrow. And then look: you see the grain-fields down yonder? I do not eat bread. Wheat is of no use to me. The wheat fields have nothing to say to me. And that is sad. But you have hair that is the color of gold. Think how wonderful that will be when you have tamed me! The grain, which is also golden, will bring me back the thought of you. And I shall love to listen to the wind in the wheat. . . ."

So the little prince tamed the fox. And when the hour of his departure drew near—

"Ah," said the fox, "I shall cry."

"It is your own fault" said the prince. "I never wished you any sort of harm; but you wanted me to tame you. . . ."

"Yes, that is so," said the fox.

"But now you are going to cry!" said the little prince.

"Yes, that is so," said the fox.

"Then it has done you no good at all!"

"It has done me good," said the fox, "because of the color of the wheat fields."[24]

I love this scene because it shows how relationships make us rich by adding meaning to our lives. The wise little fox knows this, and he knows that anything—a sound or a color—that reminds us of shared experiences adds another layer of meaning to our lives. If the fox were writing a journal for the Little Prince, he might write, "Every time I look at the wheat fields, I feel happy because they remind me of the color of your hair."

The things that connect you to your child are ties. Think about the ties that already bind the two of you together:

- Objects that remind you of shared experiences
- Idiosyncrasies he or she has that you appreciate (perhaps even share)
- Traits, qualities, habits, physical features—anything about your child that you notice and appreciate
- Nicknames your child likes to be called
- A passage from a book you read together—perhaps it is relevant to your relationship; perhaps it is simply beautiful or profound
- A line (from a movie or play or book) that you both thought was funny or insightful—perhaps you've already had occasion to quote it to each other
- An inside joke

Each tie binds you to the other person, weaving a stronger relationship and brightening the tapestry of your shared lives. Recording these threads of meaning in your journal reinforces them and gives them permanence.

---

[24] An excerpt from chapter 21 of *The Little Prince* by Antoine de Saint Exupery, translated by Katherine Woods, published by Harcourt Brace Jovanovich, New York, 1971.

It Doesn't Take Much to Blow Up the Bridge

The sad truth is that it's always easier to destroy than to build. Beautiful bridges that took years to build and required the best efforts of brilliant architects and skilled craftsmen can be destroyed in a moment by a single bomb. In the same way, building relationships requires large investments of time and creative effort; destroying them takes nothing but simple neglect or carelessness or self-centeredness or dishonesty. The destruction can happen all at once with a single bomb, or it can happen bit by bit with small wounds. But the result is so devastating that some people never muster the energy to clean up the mess and start rebuilding.

All the love and work we put into our children's journals can be negated if the way we treat our children in person or the things we say about our children to other people don't reinforce the same message of love.

Chapter 11

When Souls Get Hungry, Words Are Nourishment

*A look, a word, a tone of voice even, is often of vital
importance in the eyes of God.*
—Hannah Whitall Smith

Words as Nourishment

Yesterday morning, I spent half an hour chopping vegetables and choosing spices—filling the crock pot with all kinds of good things so that I could serve my family a healthful and tasty beef stew for supper. I'm not a gourmet chef, but every once in a while I think my family ought to have some real food for dinner so they can stay healthy and happy.

Most parents desire to nourish their children physically. We put thought and effort into providing protein and calcium and vitamins.

The Bible says that good words offer nourishment for the soul.[25] And there is plenty of negative evidence of this principle being violated: Verbal abuse or neglect damages the soul just as physical abuse or neglect damages the body.

---

[25] Proverbs 18:20–21.

Would we feed our children poison? Of course not—intentionally. But we often don't feed them as well as we could because we simply don't think about it. And we often dish out harmful words or meaningless messages when—if we simply took a minute to think—we could give them valuable nourishment.

Speaking Before We Think

Communication with our kids is so spontaneous that we often say things we never intended to say. One evening my husband, Greg, and I had to attend a meeting on a school night; we left the kids home alone (they were fifteen, thirteen, and ten). As we were driving home, I called ahead on my cell phone to be sure they were finishing all their chores: piano practicing, homework, getting ready for bed. They had been goofing around, so I scolded them and told them to hurry and get busy. After I hung up, Greg said, "Don't you think you were a little harsh—saying you're disappointed with them?" This shocked me into replaying the conversation in my mind. He was right. I had been so focused on accomplishing my mission—getting them to do their jobs—that I hadn't even thought about the way I was speaking, whether my tone and words were building them up or tearing them down.

Whenever I take the time to think before I speak, I discover that there are several ways to make the same point. Why not use a kind tone of voice?

Journaling: The Pause that Refreshes

Sometimes when we find ourselves in the midst of a confusing situation and don't know what to say to a child, the best response may be to say nothing yet. If time permits, you might want to work through the issue in your private, personal journal. But remember that even private journals may be "accidentally" read. If you write something that would be damaging if discovered, rip it out and get rid of it. There is no value in keeping those pages, though there was probably tremendous value in writing them.

Writing has the advantage of slowing you down and helping you figure out what you actually think.

Writing the Truth in Love

The ability to communicate with language is one of our distinctly human capacities, and we are responsible for how we use it. Facts may be objective, but the words we choose to label or describe those facts are always subjective. I am responsible for the words I use.

I never use the journals to scold or lecture or berate my kids, because of course then they would hate the books and not want to read them. But more important, I want to bless my children with memories that can serve as the foundation of a healthy and good life. I don't write about every event of the child's life. But I do try to include events that might have looked negative on the surface but that can be presented in a positive way. Here is an example from Britta's book, fall 2003.

BRITTA THE INVENTOR

Your Challenge: Daddy asked you to carry a pile of two x four's from the back of his truck down the hill and around to the back basement door so he can build our new project room.

Response: Most people would just pick up the wood and carry it. You thought of a way to rig up the wagon and a five-gallon pail (duct-taped together) so you could roll the wood down the hill. How brilliant you are. You will make life better for people by saving them from unnecessary toil. Many people suffer unnecessarily and need people like you to brighten their lives.

George Eliott said, "What do we live for if not to make life less difficult for each other?"

P.S. I also think it's wonderful how well you worked with Jack to be a team.

Confession: Before I wrote this entry, I was ready to pull out my hair because Britta had turned a ten-minute task into a major project. I wanted her to get done and move on to the next task. She was fully engaged with her work—giving it her whole mind and body. As I opened the garage door to tell her to hurry up, I suddenly saw her unique approach to life (which had been an irritation to me the moment before) as delightful and amusing. So I ran for my camera, took a picture of her, and then went to write it down in her book. Only as I was writing did I see the even broader implication. I could visualize this unique quality as, in fact, the seed of some future contribution to society.

Make Criticism Palatable

Children don't like to be corrected any more than they like eating broccoli, but both are essential for their development. And just as most kids don't mind veggies if they're served fresh with a tasty dip, they can also handle correction if it is worded as a specific action you want them to change. On the other hand, if a child's identity is criticized, there doesn't appear to be any hope for change. Destructive comments have the toxic effect of making negative behavior more ingrained and leading to depression and alienation.

Martin E. P. Seligman, in *The Optimistic Child*, offers an example of a positive way to criticize a child. He quotes a conversation that took place while a family was driving to the zoo.

The older child, Elena, ten, was taunting her three-year-old brother, trying to frighten him.

> Mrs. W: Elena, the teasing has got to stop. What has gotten into you today? You are such a wonderful big sister. You teach Daniel games. You share your toys. You really make him feel special. But today you haven't been nice to him at all. Zoos can be scary for little kids and your teasing him is not helping. You know I don't like this kind of behavior, Elena. I want you to apologize to Daniel, and if you tease him again today, you will not be allowed to play outside after dinner. Is that clear?[26]

Seligman says this type of criticism is effective because it gives the girl concrete evidence that the problem is fixable and that she has good reason to feel proud of herself. This criticism is effective because the mom tells her specifically what she can do in order to solve the problem: apologize and stop teasing. By way of contrast, Seligman asks us to imagine how destructive it would be if Mrs. W. had said something like this:

> Elena! I am sick of this! Why are you always such a brat? Here I plan a nice day for the three of us, and you go and ruin it! I don't know why I even bother trying to do fun family things when, without fail, you pull some stunt that spoils everything![27]

"Children absorb criticism of this sort," says Seligman, "and take away this message: 'I'm a horrible person. Mommy wishes I wasn't her daughter. I always ruin everything she does. She's

---

[26] Martin E. P. Seligman Ph.D., *The Optimistic Child* (New York: Houghton Mifflin, 1995), 65.
[27] Ibid., 66.

right. I ought to run away. They'd be better off without me.' Elena feels worthless, and the only action possible is to withdraw emotionally from the family."

As parents, we have more power than we may realize (or want). Each word we say makes our child stronger or weaker.

How does a journal come into play? In a situation like Elena's, her mother may use the journal later to reinforce Elena's success in overcoming her nasty mood. Mrs. W. might write something like this:

> Elena, you are so good at rising to a challenge. The minute I asked you to stop teasing Daniel, you were quick to apologize and think of a game to play. This is a very good example for Daniel. I hope he watches you carefully and learns how to be a good friend. I love taking you on family adventures. Wasn't it fun when the gorilla came right up to the front of its cage and made faces at us?

The point you want to make is that your child is good at learning and growing. All children try out negative behavior. It's our job to help them see three things: first, that it is ineffective; second, that there are better ways to act; and third, that they are capable of doing good things and doing them well.

Recovering from Parenting Mistakes with Good Will

Here's an entry from Britta's book in which I make a confession. I had just done a terrible job correcting her, yet she swallowed it, and her maturity was an inspiration to me.

> 5/7/04: You, my little flower, have an amazing capacity to blossom, to thrive, to profit from pruning.

This morning I went to the door to let the cats in and screamed, slamming the door shut and saying, "George tried to bring a dead bird in!" [George is one of our cats.]

You said would I please not mention gross things while you are eating breakfast.

I, still rattled, snapped, "Why is it always[28] about you? Think of my trauma opening the door!" or something rude like that. Britta, I'm so sorry! But you graciously apologized and sat stunned in your chair, pondering. A few minutes later, when I asked what snacks you wanted to put in your school bag to eat before softball practice, you said you wanted two things: 1) goldfish crackers and 2) not to be self-centered.

Your humility inspires me. You are able to benefit from my criticism even when I'm not able to deliver it very well. I want to be like you, so full of life that nothing stops me, so healthy and well balanced that nothing knocks me over, so flexible I can bend, not break, so full of good will that I can recycle any trash anyone throws at me and profit from it.

You and I are Goodwill Girls.

P.S. May I have a receipt for that?

The Goodwill theme is one of the recurring threads in my discussions with Britta. There is a Goodwill store nearby, and when we have a pile of old clothes or other things the family no longer can use, we give it to the Goodwill people to recycle and sell for a profit. They give us a tax-deductible receipt. We

---

[28] Martin Seligman would be very troubled by my use of the word *always*. So am I. We should make our criticism limited and specific—focusing on one, changeable behavior. I certainly should have taken a minute to think before speaking. But Britta survived.

find it amazing that what is junk to us is valuable to them. And this inspires us to take "junk" such as insults that people throw at us and find ways to profit from them.

The first time Britta and I talked about this, I was driving her to an early-morning piano lesson. She was telling me about some rude kids at school who said not-very-nice things. I presented the Goodwill analogy, and she laughed and said the next time someone says something rude to her, she'll say, "Do you want a receipt for that?" This little joke has done wonders to help keep both of us optimistic.

If We Don't Nourish Their Souls, Who Will?

Betsy said yesterday that when she came home from school the house smelled good. She liked that there was stew in the crock pot. If I hadn't taken half an hour earlier in the day to chop those vegetables, my family would have found something to eat—probably at a fast-food restaurant. And that's not tragic (we do it frequently enough). But I think I can do better than that.

There are plenty of days when I unthinkingly spout out careless words to my children, which isn't tragic either. But my goal is to do better than that. I want to nourish my children's souls, and journals function as something of a "crock pot" to facilitate that goal.

Chapter 12

"Publishing" Promotes the Positive

> *How wonderful it is that nobody need wait a single minute*
> *before starting to improve the world.*
> —Anne Frank

Anne Frank, through her diary, has done much to improve the world—though she had no way of knowing at the time how many lives her written words would touch. When she wrote the above quotation, I don't suppose she was thinking in particular of her own diary, but about simple moment-by-moment choices we make that either build or destroy goodness around us. That is the positive spirit reflected in her diary, which was found and published by her father after Anne's death. That beautiful and hopeful spirit is one of the reasons her diary has had such a positive impact on generations of readers.

The journal you keep for your child may never be published, but in the life of at least one Very Important Person it can have the same powerful and positive impact. Anything written in a book is, in one sense, "published." It is made permanent and set out on a page to be read and reread. It becomes the focus of attention.

All the News that's Fit to Print

Some reporters like to dig up dirt. They're quick to publish scandals and "scoops"—anything that promotes sales.

I'm interested in promoting character growth, so I'm on a mission to spot evidence of anything positive that might be growing in the lives of my kids. When I see something good, I write it down in the journal.

The Power of Selection

Newspapers and magazines, even those that claim to be unbiased, slant the news simply by printing some stories and omitting others. There's no way around it. Space is limited. Choices must be made. Each story, each bit of news, is evaluated in terms of its relevance and importance. The editor decides whether to print it, how much space to give it, and how prominently to place it. Putting it on the front page along with a large photo causes the story to receive lots of attention and thereby impacts how a community understands itself. Tucking the story into a three-inch space on page seven almost guarantees that the story will have a negligible impact on readers.

You are one of the editors of your child's life story. Even if you don't want this responsibility, it's yours. Even if you're not writing a journal for your child, you function in this role. Everything your child does and says, everything that happens in your child's life—these are the "stories." You decide which ones will be given prominent place in your attention and your memory. The way you talk or write about that event determines the "angle" and creates a frame for the story. Every time you retell the story, you increase its prominence.

Putting words on paper harnesses, intensifies, and sharpens the power of attention. Keeping a journal helps me to be more intentional about using that power.

Actively Promoting Goodness

James says, "The wise are peacemakers who go on quietly sowing for a harvest of righteouness—in other people and in themselves" (James 3:18; Phillips). This is a lovely (if idyllic) image of parenting: We sow words of faith and hope and love into our children, and a harvest of righteousness blossoms. But we're talking about reality here. Parents need to deal with kids as they really are. Some days we take the role of peacemaker; other days we must do battle against the forces of evil that want to destroy our kids.

J. R. R. Tolkein's trilogy *The Lord of the Rings* offers us a picture of the proper relationship between war and peace. The purpose of war is to protect peace. In Tolkein's story, the fight to destroy the Ring must be fought so that good community life, represented by the Shire, can continue. The only reason Frodo and Sam and the others risk their lives fighting against evil is to protect their villages and their families. Their courage and self-sacrifice are noble virtues. The faithfulness and consistency of the people who kept ordinary life thriving back in the Shire are also virtues.

Earth is a war zone. Battles between good and evil might spring up at any time, and we are frequently called upon to defend the kingdom of God. If you are in the midst of a battle, I pray God will give you a quick victory. If you are not engaged in battle, I hope you are living in the Shire—actively sowing seeds of righteousness in others and yourself by speaking and writing words that promote and protect the good, the true, and the beautiful within your family and your community.

Some personalities thrive on the excitement of battle. The thrill of conflict brings out their best character qualities. Daily family life, on the other hand, with all its repetition and ordinariness and tiresome duties, lulls them into carelessness. Remember that your home is the Shire. It is the reason all the battles are fought and all journeys undertaken—so that children will have a safe and good place in which to blossom into the idea God had in mind when He created them.

How to Identify Positive Qualities

It's important for us to be able to identify qualities worth encouraging in our children. Sometimes children display virtues that we don't recognize because they are out of balance or used inappropriately. In situations like this it would be easy to damage a child's potential good. For example, my middle child is very creative, which is certainly a positive quality. But this creativity often "creates" big messes or distracts her from doing other important things or sends her brain off in unconventional directions. If I weren't careful, I could discipline that creativity right out of her. My challenge is to keep the positive quality alive while coaching her about appropriate ways and times to express it.

I've heard it said that every weakness is a strength out of balance. When our children display negative qualities, our job is to discover the inverse strength and help them learn how to manage their gifts. A spendthrift has the capacity to be generous. An obsessively neat child can be well ordered. One who has trouble being on time can be flexible. Look for evidence of these positive qualities and highlight them in your child's journal. Don't give the out-of-balance qualities any press at all.

The Power of Enjoyment

When a child misbehaves in public—in some clever or precocious way—the parents are always quick to say to spectators, "Don't laugh, or I'll never be able to get him to stop doing it!"

To enjoy your child's behavior is to affirm it. And to affirm it is to ensure its repetition.

Your children love to know they are the source of your delight. People of all ages find happiness in being able to give happiness. It's human nature. When you are able to enjoy your child, you not only increase your own joy you fulfill one of your child's deepest longings. On top of that, you increase the amount of overall joy in the world, which can only be good. Expressing that joy in a journal helps you be intentional about taking delight in your child and allows you to sharpen your joy by articulating it.

The Significance of Expectations

Just as children by nature want to please people, they also tend to meet expectations—if those expectations are clearly spelled out. Meeting expectations is one way to please people, after all. This aspect of human nature was illustrated in a fascinating experiment conducted by two Princeton University psychologists, John Darley and Daniel Batson.[29] The study was inspired by the biblical story of the good Samaritan. In the story told by Jesus, a traveler who has been beaten and robbed is left on the side of the road for dead. Various people pass by and avoid him, but finally a Samaritan (a member of a despised minority) comes along and cares for the man.

In the recently conducted experiment, seminary students were asked to prepare a short message on a biblical theme, then walk to a different building to present it. Along the way to that building, they had to walk past a man slumped in an alley with his head down, coughing and groaning. The question was, Who would stop to help the man?

---

[29] As reported by Malcolm Gladwell in *The Tipping Point: How Little Things Can Make a Big Difference* (Boston: Little, Brown and Company. 2000).

There were three variables. First, some were asked to speak on the parable of the good Samaritan while others were given a different subject. In the end, this didn't make a difference in determining whether people stopped. The second variable was personal motivation. Before the experiment, the subjects were given a survey to find out why they were preparing for ministry: Did they want personal spiritual fulfillment or did they want a practical tool for finding meaning in everyday life? It turned out there was no correlation between the way they answered that question and whether they stopped to help the man in need. Here's what made a difference: Some of the students, as they left to go to the second building, were told, "You're late. They were expecting you a few minutes ago. You'd better get moving." Others were told, "It will be a few minutes before they're ready for you, but you might as well head over now." Of those who were told they were late, only 10 percent stopped to help. Of those who thought they had time to spare, 63 percent stopped. The voice of someone telling them they were expected to be somewhere in a hurry had the power to override a competing value—in this case, compassion.

As parents, we need to think carefully about what values we stress, because our children will tend to prioritize those same values.

Some Sample Stories

One summer our family vacation consisted of a week in a rented fishing cabin near the Canadian border. Betsy was a bit disappointed we weren't traveling someplace interesting (with, for example, white sand, sunshine, sprawling shopping malls, and a nearby Jamba Juice). I could sympathize, knowing there wouldn't be a Starbucks within biking distance. But I encouraged both of us to be open to a new kind of adventure.

She was hesitant, but I was on the lookout for positive growth that I could nurture, and it soon came. This is what I wrote.

> 6/9/03. At Idlewild Resort, Lake Kabatogama:
> Julia Cameron says, "The quality of our lives is in proportion, always, to the capacity for delight. The capacity for delight is the gift of paying attention."[30]
> You are very capable of delight even when something trips you up a bit (you weren't sure you could enjoy a week at a cabin fishing, for example).
> You recover well.
> You paid attention, kept an open mind and heart, and soon saw your way clear. You perceived the fun in fishing and embraced it wholeheartedly.
> Last night you and Jack and Daddy stayed out in the cold and rain with Jerry the guide—catching saugers and walleyes (yours was 22¼ inches—just outside the slot!) until after 10:00. You came in glowing.
> This morning you read a few pages of *Silas Marner* while Dad and I made bacon and French toast. You came to the table saying, "I like this place." (Having to do dishes almost made you change your mind, but you've recovered already ☺.)

This is from Britta's book, January 1996. She was five.

> You really have mastered the art of living! When I told you we couldn't go to ballet class because the roads were too icy, you put on your saddest face and

---

[30] Julia Cameron, *The Artist's Way: A Spiritual Path to Higher Creativity* (New York: G. P. Putnam's Sons), 53. I know I've quoted this in her journal before. Repetition is an effective teaching tool, so I never hesitate to repeat wisdom.

gave me a big hug. Then you caught your breath and said, "I know! If there are no other cars on the road, we won't crash into anyone." After I assured you that your solution was creative but impractical, you tried again. "I know, Mom. We can have a tea party—just you and me." That was just the thing the afternoon called for!

Almost three years later, I wrote this in Britta's book, 12/8/98. She was eight.

> One of the reasons Mother Teresa was so effective for God was that she learned at a young age to "greet poverty and adversity with an enterprising spirit." (Charlotte Grey wrote this in her biography of Mother Teresa. It's a good book. I hope you read it someday.)
> I see in you, my beloved Britta, an enterprising spirit. Last night at supper, Jack was paralyzed because his hot dog had too much ketchup. He didn't want to eat it that way so he sat and stared at it. Once you noticed his dilemma, you jumped right in with a solution. Problems never look like road blocks to you. You treat them as interesting detours or as an obstacle course.

One important aspect of parenting is teaching children that thoughts are a choice and that each of us is responsible for the thoughts we choose.

An ideal teaching situation is when a child discovers some aspect of truth on her own and you can record it in her journal as an anchor to steady her during later storms. Not only is she more open to truth that she has discovered herself, but she will come to see herself as her own teacher. This is one of the keys to lifelong learning—not to depend on others to set up learning situations for you but to develop the skill of unpacking experience and pulling out the gifts of knowledge and insight.

Here's an insight Britta had when she was seven. It's one of those simple truths that children tend to understand better than adults. As her life becomes more complicated and fear attacks more subtly, the record of her childlike trust may steady her.

3/13/98. I walked through the living room as you were watching a Veggie Tales movie called something like, "Where Is God When I'm Scared?" You said, "Mom, you know why we don't have to worry about bad things happening to us? Because God made us, and if He wanted us, it's His job to take care of us. Just like Betsy wanted a hamster, so it's her job to take care of it. Good thing I watched this movie or I wouldn't have known that."

Britta, you have a marvelous sense of spiritual truth and a good mind for analogies. You understand ownership and what it means to be owned by God. Your dad says you're going to grow up to be a theologian. I think a saint.

Our son Jack's full name is Jonathan. One of his favorite stories is about King David and his best friend Jonathan. In the following journal entry I am "publishing" the fact that he is living up to his namesake.

8/20/03. How well you live up to your name—a true friend (as Jonathan was to David). Today you told me you are eager to invite Peter to do something with you right away so he won't feel bad about backing out of the overnight. Yesterday he accepted your invitation to sleep over, but ended up calling his mom about 10:00 and going home because he gets nervous sleeping away from home. Some boys might have teased him. Others might have liked him less. Your response to his weakness was to be a strength to him, to affirm your friendship. I count myself blessed to be among your friends.

We try to protect our children from evil, but we cannot protect them forever. Soon we must explain that evil is real, that people have free will and often choose to mess up the good world God has created and continues to build. Our job is to join the good side and do everything in our power to promote good and stop evil. Children can do this, too, in increasingly significant ways. We can coach them to do this and praise them whenever we see them doing it. Here's an example from Betsy's book, 5/27/03.

How bold and compassionate you are! Saving a baby bunny from the mouth of George [our cat]! You heard it scream and ran right out to rescue it, then brought it in to care for it. You shared it with Britta, who has been praying and begging for a bunny, then [you both decided to] let it go back to its mother and its home.

You are God's hand of intervention to stop evil and promote goodness.[31] God trained David to rescue the Israelites by teaching him to rescue sheep from the mouths of lions.

It might sound melodramatic or pretentious to you—to look at ordinary children doing small things and see heroes saving the world, but children thrive on it. And the truth is that all great people started out as small children, and their small

---

[31] I realize that one animal preying on another isn't moral evil, but Betsy thought it was, so this worked as an example for her. We have to use examples that are real for our children.

actions prepared them for the bigger actions they would take later. Just so, our children's actions will determine who they become. My goal is to encourage them to identify themselves as active promoters of goodness and fighters against evil.

Chapter 13

Your Journal Inspires Your Child to Read

It is through the imagination that we can escape the
narrowness of our own experience.
—American philosopher Russell Kirk
paraphrased by Wesley McDonald

You Can Be Your Child's Favorite Author

If your child is a reluctant reader, try writing a simple story about some special event that he or she enjoys reliving. Most children are fascinated by the story of the day they were born, for example. It was, after all, their very first adventure. Write what happened, in large print and in language that is at or slightly above your child's reading level. Keep it simple, with only one or two sentences per page. You can illustrate the pages with photos or drawings. Your child could be the illustrator. Fairy-tale language can add color: "Once upon a time, in the land of _____, a prince (or princess) was born. . . ."

Stories like this could be written in a separate book or in a journal you have already started for your child—just write the title on the next empty page and carry on. Don't worry about the journal's overall chronological order.

Don't Wait until Your Child Can Read

The preschool years are the most crucial years for language development. As you read to and talk with your children, you are helping them understand how language works and what words mean. This is essential preparation for learning how to read. Even basic concepts, such as the facts that words are read from left to right on a page and that books are read from front to back, need to be taught. Your journal can be one of the books you read to your child as you sit and rock together.

The Journal as a Reading Log

Another way your journal can encourage your child to read is by serving as a reading log. You might want to use the back page of the journal as a place to list all the books your child reads. This will give your child a healthy sense of accomplishment and be a happy reminder of hours well spent.

An alternate strategy is to give each child a separate Reading Journal. I have one for each of my kids and encourage them to use one page per book to record the title, author, the date they finished reading it, one quotation, the theme in one sentence, and a plot summary in a couple of sentences. Unfortunately, I'm not good at being consistent with this project. During one summer I "paid" them for each book report, but even then they didn't always bother to write them up. You may be more successful than I am. Anyway, I figure that even the few reports that got written were educational. And we can always pick up the project again in the future.

We can't keep everything going all the time. Good projects are good even if you only do them one day.

The Journal as a Record of Shared Books

One type of entry I like to make in my kids' journals consists of a quotation from a book we are reading together and a comment about it—maybe the fact that it made us laugh or cry or we thought it was beautiful or it reminded us of something. An entry can be as simple as this one in Betsy's book. We were (still) working our way through an abridged version of *Les Miserables*. Eponine is Betsy's favorite character in the story. We had just read the chapter in which she got shot. The entry is simply this:

6/24/04. Last night Eponine died. We sat at the kitchen table and cried and cried.

Some entries include a quotation from the book along with some connection to family life:

Betsy's journal, 1/4/05. On New Year's Day you and I spent some time in the afternoon reading chapter 8 of *Silas Marner*.[32] Here's your favorite quote: "Instead of trying to still his [Godfrey's] fears he encouraged them, with that superstitious impression which clings to us all, that if we expect evil very strongly it is the less likely to come."

On the drive home from Frontier Steak House later that night, after celebrating the new year with Popi and Grammy, you told Dad to be careful driving on the icy roads but added that expecting an accident very strongly wouldn't keep it from happening.

You are so good at applying wisdom to practical daily life!

---

[32] See Appendix, p. 155.

Entries about books reinforce the fact that reading is an important part of our lives, and the stories we read together are threads in the tapestry of shared family culture.

Chapter 14

A Legacy Can Make a Difference for a Lifetime

When you speak, your words echo only across the room.
But when you write, your words echo down the ages.
—Bud Gardner

Years from now your child may need to read exactly what you have to say today. Generations from now, your grandchild may be strengthened and encouraged by the investment of thought and time you are making today. But long before that, you yourself may be grateful for the treasured moments you took time to preserve on paper.

Life Is Unpredictable

I'm typing this through tears because this morning my college roommate called to tell me her surgery was "successful," but that the cancer was diagnosed as stage 3, and she only has a 50 percent chance of living for five years. The truth is that none of us knows how many more days we have on this earth.

Another friend of mine, April, has started keeping journals for her children because her own mother died when April was only four. One of the deepest longings of April's heart is to know who her mother was, what she thought about life and about her little girl.

American poet Edna St. Vincent Millay died when she was only fifty eight. She never had children, but she had a sense that her writing was the legacy she would leave this world. Her poem "Journal" begins with these lines:

> This book when I am gone will be
> A little faint perfume of me.

Memories as Treasures

Last summer I decided to read through the journals I had been keeping for the kids. I came across this entry I had written when Jack was three.

> As I was tucking your flannel shirt into your blue jeans, you took my face in your dimpled little hands, gave me a sweet kiss on my lips, and said, "Me kiss you. You happy now?"
>
> Then you did a little fake cry and said, "You kiss me." My kiss brought a smile and a "Me happy now. You sad now?"
>
> "Okay," I said, doing a little fake cry so you could kiss me and make me "happy now!"
>
> Back and forth a dozen times.
>
> The gift of this moment I will treasure in my heart all my life.

I wanted to treasure it and specifically intended to treasure it. But only six years later, I had completely forgotten it. What if I hadn't written it down? How many other moments have I missed? I've sometimes gone a year without writing anything. It took me ten years to fill my first journal. But there is no profit in regretting unrecorded memories. Much better to use that energy recording current thoughts. Remember what Eleanor Roosevelt said when she was asked how she accomplished so much: "I don't have any more time than anybody else. I just don't waste any of it on regrets." The truth is that even if I had recorded only that one event, it would be a priceless treasure worth savoring with gratitude. And if the only journaling you ever do is to take ten minutes right now to record one good thought or memory of your child, that will be something to feel very good about.

Journals as Timely Gifts

Another way in which a journal can work as a legacy is that it can hold safe your words of love and wisdom until the time when your child is ready to hear them. How much love is given but not received because the recipient is preoccupied or confused or simply not ready to receive it? How much wisdom is lost on children whose inexperience (or attitude problem) prevents them from grasping its significance? Writing can mediate these situations.

I've had the wonderful experience (you probably have too) of rereading a book that I had thoroughly enjoyed and felt sure I understood years before, only to see it differently and enjoy whole layers of meaning I had missed the first time. Age and experience sharpen our minds so we can dig out riches that are buried deep within stories (the ones we experience as well as the ones we read).

Here are a few lines I copied into my son's journal from a book called *The Silver Chair*, which he and I read together when he was nine.

"Friends," said the prince, "when once a man is launched on such an adventure as this, he must bid farewell to hopes and fears, otherwise death or deliverance will both come too late to save his honor and his reason."[32]

The concept here is mighty deep for a nine-year-old boy, yet at some level Jack grasped it enough to be attracted to the bravery expressed. As he grows older and faces more adventures, he will be able to understand it more fully.

Choosing a Positive Legacy

Many families have lively oral traditions—stories they repeat whenever relatives gather. Unfortunately, some of these stories have the tragic effect of opening old wounds or keeping mistakes alive or replaying hurtful memories. In the journal you are writing, you have the power to select only those stories that will build a positive legacy.

---

[32] C. S. Lewis, *The Silver Chair*, 193.

Chapter 15

Purposeful Giving ॐ

It is necessary to write, if the days are not to slip emptily by.
How else, indeed, to clap the net over the butterfly of this moment?
—Vita Sackville-West[33]

The Courage to Be a Parent

Parenting is difficult. This is the first and most understated truth of parenting. And the second is like it: Parenting is painful. Shall I continue? Parenting can be lonely—even if you and your spouse do it as a team or have supportive friends, and even if you have wonderfully close times with your child. There are times you feel alone. Not only this; Parenting is unsettling. You can't always know exactly what to do next. You may not be sure how to understand what's going on. The relationships are always fluctuating. Every hour the variables rearrange themselves. Questions come without warning. Answers elude you, and help is hard to find. What works for your friends with their kids might not work in your house with your kids. What worked with one child might not work with the next child at the same age.

---

[33] Quoted by Garrison Keillor in the Writer's Almanac, 2004.

Yes, there are principles. But how do I apply that general wisdom right now with this particular child who has never been this exact age before, facing this new situation with variables I never could have predicted? Even when I'm confident about what to say or do in a given situation, it may not "work"; that is, my children may misinterpret or thwart my efforts to lovingly guide them.

Courage is what we need.

A wise person once said, "Courage is the quality of mind and spirit that enables me to deal with pain and difficulty." I like this definition because packed inside it is the secret to being courageous: *Deal with it.* Face it. Don't run away. Don't escape or mentally check out. Stay there, with your child. Stay engaged.

That having been said, there are, of course, times when you need to get away in order to clear your thoughts and restore your sense of balance and sanity. You need to spend time with people who encourage you; you need an identity apart from being your child's parent.

Sandra Felton offers insightful advice to people who face challenging family relationships: "Give less attention to the problem and more attention to the business of living fully. Nothing is so compelling to encourage others toward rational living as the presence of a healthy, vibrant force in the home. As you turn your attention away from the problem and toward strengthening yourself in body, mind, and spirit, you may be surprised at the influence you have."[34] This kind of "getting away" is not running away. It is necessary self-encouragement: preparing yourself to face the pain and difficulty. For me it might mean going for a walk or a swim at the health club. It means planning a date to have coffee with a friend. It means announcing to my family (on a relatively free evening when no one urgently needs me), "No one talk to me for an hour—I'm having a read." Most

---

[34] Sandra Felton, *When You Live with a Messie* (Grand Rapids, MI: Baker. 1994) 192.

important, it means that on most days I get up early so I can read a chapter of my Bible, pray, and write in my journal before I need to deal with the business of the day.

Don't Let Problems Consume You

Does it seem counter-intuitive to say that the best way to deal with a problem might be by *not* focusing on it right now? I'm not suggesting living in an illusion or ignoring reality. I am suggesting that we keep our lives balanced and not let problems take more attention than they deserve. When we become obsessed with fixing something, our intense focus makes the problem loom so large that it seems to be the only reality.

In a recent talk on family life, Mark Wolbert said, "Growth comes from building on talents and gifts, not from solving problems."[35] Taking this approach not only frees us of the burden to fix our kids, it also breathes new life into the relationship by allowing us to enjoy all the things our children are doing well.

Sometimes I use the journals I keep for my kids to sidestep a conflict and reconnect with my child circuitously. I remember a time when I was upset about something Betsy was doing. The next day, while she was at school, I wrote in her journal about something completely unrelated, something sweet she had done. It helped me reconnect with my positive feelings toward her so I could isolate my negative feelings about the issue. The next time the thorny issue came up, I was prepared to listen to her reasons and articulate my concerns, and we came to a consensus we could both live with.

Enjoying the Available Good

I remember when I was about eight months pregnant with my first child. I was feeling heavy, uncomfortable, impatient,

---

[35] New Life Christian Center, Princeton, Minnesota, December 5, 2004.

and scared. But my friend Faye, who had recently given birth to her second child, gave me some powerful advice. She said, "*Love* your time in the hospital." I wasn't sure what she was talking about at first. But she explained to me that as soon as I got home from the hospital, there would be much to do, and *I* would have to do it. It would be worse, she warned, if I had more than one child. "But your time in the hospital is just for you," she said. "Let them pamper you. Let the nurses take care of you and bring you meals. Just soak in all their care. Don't be anxious to get home. Rest. Think of it as a vacation."

Amazingly, I was allowed five days in the hospital: I had an unexpected C-section, and back in 1988 that meant my insurance company paid for five days. I'm sure if Faye hadn't coached me, I would have felt trapped there. It would have seemed like an interruption, and I would have been impatient to get home. But I remembered what she said and cherished those days, just cuddling my baby and enjoying visits from my husband and friends. I still have the souvenir coffee mug the staff gave me as I was leaving, and every time I drink out of it, I have happy memories of that delightful island in time.

Faye spoke with the voice of experience and as someone looking back on an opportunity missed. Have you heard the same voice? It often comes from parents whose children are older than ours and who look back on a happiness that was fleeting, on opportunities to have their lives complicated by needy little ones who offer us their hearts. Empty-nesters tell us to *love* this time when our children are still with us. When we realize how precious this season of life is, we want to do just that, but hardly know how. Journaling is one very good way, because we can use it to focus our attention on the available good.

Every day is an island of time. It presents us with challenges and opportunities, but in limited quantities. No one day ever holds every possible good, so it's always tempting to focus on the good that isn't here now.

You might want to use your personal journal to list—each day—five good things that are available for you to enjoy, then be sure to thoroughly enjoy them. They might not be here tomorrow. Some days we have our health; other days we don't. Some days our children fill us with delight; other days they cause us pain. Today the financial stress might seem unbearable, but your relationships might be rewarding. Or you may be suffering from loneliness but find yourself in beautiful surroundings. No one gets every possible good at every moment.

There are people who look like they have it all. But their closest friends will tell you that they still find things to complain about; they are still tempted to want something they don't have. This is human nature. But human nature is also free. We can choose to enjoy the available good right now. Whatever stage of life you're at, whatever age your children are, won't last. This moment is precious. You only get to live this day once. Let your journal inspire you to notice how full of grace it is.

Parenting with Paper

Writing to your child is not better than spending time with your child. But there are moments when you can't be with your child, or you don't need to be with your child. In fact, as in the above example, there are moments when the best thing you can do is be away from your child. You know these moments.

Sometimes I can think about my child better from a distance. I can see the beautiful soul shining through the unpolished behavior. I can take time to choose my words more carefully. Writing is slower than talking and allows for more thoughtful (and uninterrupted) responses.

Teachable Moments

Flashes of insight, moments of connectedness, displays of noble attitudes—these are priceless little epiphanies in the life of your child. Your journal can preserve them by documenting them, putting a frame around the moment to set it off and accentuate its significance.

Here's an entry I wrote in Betsy's journal in October of 2004 after we spent a Saturday night at home alone together. The others in our family were all out doing interesting things, but we had no plans and both needed to do chores. In the beginning of this entry I make a reference to the five elements of fiction because Betsy was, at that time, studying short stories in English and would frequently read whatever story she was studying aloud to me in the evenings, so *plot, characters, setting, point of view,* and *theme* were familiar words in our vocabulary.

Betsy, you've learned from experience that *who you're with* affects the quality of life more than *where you are.* The *characters* matter more than the *setting* of a story.

I think the characters matter more than the *plot* as well. For example, Saturday night you and I were the only ones home. We both had chores to do, but because we were happy to be together, the chores furnished us with a plot around which to enjoy each other's company.

First I cut a few hydrangea flowers (while you opened your window and put one of our favorite CDs on). Then you brought out the camera out and we took a few artsy photos. We came inside and had tea and cookies (made by you and Britta and Gabi the night before) and a little chat. Then you cleaned your room while I swept and washed the kitchen floor and vacuumed my office. You read your homework short story to me while I ironed.

A lovely evening.

The setting and the plot were ordinary, but the characters were very enjoyable, and the theme was the best: *Staying home to do chores can be cozy and enjoyable when we do it together.*

When Betsy read this entry, she wrote this at the bottom of the page:

> I love you so much, Mom! The evening was very lovely. I wouldn't trade this past weekend for any other. Thanks for a great friendship. I love you. Betsy.

Oh, that parenting could always be this rewarding! Of course it isn't, but relishing and documenting the rich moments can see us through lean times.

The Right Kind of Giving

As parents, we naturally want to give everything we can to our children. And we're usually willing to make sacrifices to do so. For example, because we want to provide for our children financially, we do our best to avoid bad investments or worthless expenditures. Kids can have strong opinions about how they want us to spend our money. Love requires that we think carefully about our children's needs, now and in the future, before agreeing to give them what they think they want right now.

Time and attention are also limited and valuable resources. We want to give them to our children, but some activities simply squander these limited assets.

Anne Morrow Lindbergh, in *Gift from the Sea,* her classic exploration of what it means to be a woman and a mother, says this:

> Here is a strange paradox. Woman instinctively wants to give, yet resents giving herself in small pieces. . . . I believe that what woman resents is not so much giving herself in pieces as giving herself purposelessly. What we fear is not so much that our energy may be leaking away through small outlets as that it may be going "down the drain."

Purposeful giving is not as apt to delete one's resources; it belongs to the natural order of giving that
seems to renew itself even in the act of depletion. The
more one gives, the more one has to give—like milk in
the breast.[36]

Keeping a journal is, for me, "purposeful giving."

"Are You Listening to Me?"

It's easy for our kids to tune out our words. Especially if they
think we're going to scold or correct them. And we are certainly
obliged to correct them at times. But if we lose their attention,
we lose our influence, so we must weigh our words carefully.

Actually, our own desire to have our children listen to us
is a clue to what our children, like all people, want and need:
They want us to listen to them. As Stephen Covey says, "To feel
understood is the deepest hunger of the human soul, just as air
is the deepest hunger of the human body." If our children need
to feel understood as deeply as they need to breathe, we had
better do our best to meet that need. The first step is to give our
full attention to listening to them when they are willing to talk
with us. A further step is to journal about what we learn from
listening to them. This extra effort to process and record what we
understand about our children says that we value them highly.

You may find that by giving your attention to your child,
you have won your child's attention back. Most kids will read
very attentively if they are the subject of the writing. If you
knew that I could see good things in you that you didn't even
realize were there, wouldn't your curiosity compel you to find
out what I had to say?

---

[36] Lindbergh, Anne Morrow. *Gift from the Sea.* New York: Pantheon Books.
1992. p. 40–41.

Obviously, your child's journal will not be the only avenue of communication between the two of you—nor the primary avenue. But it will be an avenue. A positive avenue. Perhaps a well-traveled avenue. Any good communication improves your communication in general.

I read someplace that the number-one influence on kids' self-image is what they think their parents think about them. Not what you actually think, but what your kids think you think. Your kids believe you because they know that of all the people in the world, you know them best. So if you write a book about your child, you will become your child's favorite author. And what you write will be believed.

Chapter 16

Writing Rewards the Writer

And now the page beckons. Thin as a layer of silver that makes a mirror reflect, it urges, Set down here what you saw, and you will understand it as never before. And so will all the world.
—Bonnie Friedman[37]

Writing is its own reward. It enriches life and helps us realize what we value. It also helps us see how we are interpreting reality.

An Acquirable Taste

Perhaps you like the idea of writing; you can see that it would be meaningful, but you don't have a natural taste for it. It doesn't seem to be immediately satisfying. In fact, it strikes you as sheer hard work. But you are open to considering it.

Good. I think your best plan is to simply start writing. You might have to reward yourself. (E.g., don't let yourself check your e-mail until you've written a journal entry—even a one-line entry counts.) I expect that soon you will develop a taste for the

---

[37] Bonnie Friedman, *Writing Past Dark* (New York: HarperPerennial, 1994.)

writing and start to enjoy it. Have you ever trained yourself to like something you didn't like before (the taste of coffee, spicy food, watching football games, gardening)? It's not hard to do. I now look forward to going to exercise classes at the fitness center. It's still hard to overcome inertia and actually get up and go, but it helps to focus on how great I'll feel during the ten-minute cool-down at the end and for the rest of the day. With your journal, focus on how great it will feel to have written, how happy your child will be to see what you wrote, and how fun it will be to reread the entries years from now.

Writing Can Help You Realize What You Value

One day while I was out getting the mail, my neighbor drove by and stopped to chat a minute. I asked how her beauty shop was doing, and she said business was good. Too good, truth be told. As she drove off, she lamented, "I have no life."

What did she mean by that? Apparently her business, even though it was thriving, didn't give her something she wanted. What do people want if not success? I think we want meaningful relationships. The fact that her business was taking all her time meant she had no time for people.

Seventy percent of Americans between twenty and thirty years old say they would take a pay cut to spend more time with their families.[38] The other day I heard a radio announcer report that the majority of people surveyed would rather have more time off work than a $5,000 raise. Working to make a living sometimes seems to get in the way of the life we are trying to support.

Our careers are not the only threat to our lives. Even the business and the busy-ness of parenting—all the work of organizing schedules and running a home—can blur our vision. How can we redeem the days? "How we spend our days is, after all, how we spend our lives," says Annie Dillard.

---

[38] As reported in *Men's Journal*, November 2004.

Journaling, either for ourselves or for our children, is one way to be more intentional about how we spend our lives. The activity of writing keeps us awake, forcing us to pay attention to the way we did, in fact, spend our day. Did we waste it or live it? Squander it or invest it? Reject it or receive it? Resent it or embrace it?

Used this way, journaling is just what Stephen Covey claims: a "high leverage" activity. The time you spend journaling more than pays for itself by helping you realize how you want to approach the rest of your time.

Writing Can Increase Your Delight in Daily Life

The journal is like a camera. It can help you frame a situation. When I'm traveling, I keep my camera handy. My general approach to whatever I experience is, "This may be camera-worthy." I'm scanning for local color. I expect to see "sights"—things worth seeing and remembering.

Keeping a journal adds this element of attentiveness to daily life. We are pilgrims having adventures. Our children are our fellow travelers. Difficulties along the way are par for the course. What matters is how we understand the difficulty, how we respond to it, how we grow from it. The genius of the journal is that by recording your understanding, your response, and your growth, you effectively call forth truer understanding, higher responses, healthier growth.

The play *Our Town*, by Thorton Wilder, is about the glory of ordinary life. Actually, it's about how easy it is to go through life without noticing this glory.

In the story, one of the main characters has died but has the opportunity to go back to relive one day. She chooses her twelfth birthday. But she cannot make it through the day—it is too painful for her to see her family plodding through the day without really noticing how precious it is to be alive and together as a family.

Emily, in a loud voice to the stage manager, says, "I can't go on. It goes so fast. We don't have time to look at one another." She breaks down sobbing. . . . "I didn't realize. So all that was going on and we never noticed. Take me back—up the hill—to my grave. But first: Wait! One more look.

"Good by, Good by, world. Good-by . . . Mama and Papa. Good by to clocks ticking . . . and Mama's sunflowers. And food and coffee. And new-ironed dresses and hot baths . . . and sleeping and waking up. Oh, earth, you're too wonderful for anybody to realize you.

"Do any human beings ever realize life while they live it? Every, every minute?"

STAGE MANAGER: "No." Pause. "The saints and poets, maybe—they do some."

—Act III

I think the stage manager is right. Saints realize the glory of life on earth because they see it from God's point of view. Poets do because they write, and writing has a way of sharpening our focus. As parents, we can strive to do both. We can choose to see life from God's point of view, and we can write.

C. S. Lewis suggests that we can increase the "thickness" of our sense of time as we pass through it by learning to attend to more than one thing at once.[39] The more things we notice and enjoy, the richer the moment. To reflect on the meaning of what we observe enriches us by adding another layer to life. Writing facilitates this process by training us to focus both our attention and our thoughts.

Writing Can Center You

Here is an entry from my personal journal:

---

[39] C. S. Lewis, *Letters to Malcolm Chiefly on Prayer: Reflections on the Intimate Dialogue Between Man and God* (New York: Harcourt, 1992), 109.

Why does writing feel so satisfying? Why do I crave it? A page is a place to rest, to let the mind settle, to put a stop to anxiety, to get a grip on something of reality. Writing slows life down to the pace of a sentence—one word at a time. Then it can be faced, accepted, understood. And somehow the page accepts and understands me, receives me hospitably, as a friend.

Writing Can Help You Solve Problems

Research has shown that the act of writing causes people to have ideas they didn't have before they started writing. The mental effort of putting thoughts into sentences and writing those sentences down somehow forces the brain to make new connections. The insight might come from seeing what we have written, or perhaps from seeing a connection between two different things we have written.

For example, one day I was writing in my journal about my frustration with Betsy's desire to spend so much time online chatting with her friends. On the next page of my journal I was lamenting that I don't have enough time to get the yard and garden looking their best. Then—right there within those two problems on the pages of my journal, I saw how they could solve each other. I made a deal with Betsy that she could trade time spent helping me in the garden for time online chatting to her friends. She scowled but agreed (gardening is not to her taste). But after several sessions of working together outside, she began to develop a taste for it. And her cheerful company greatly eased the burden of the job for me.[40]

---

[40] This "deal" only lasted a few weeks. After that she got so busy with I-forget-which-project that she didn't have time for either the computer or the garden. When that season passed, she just asked for the computer when she wanted it. I let her have it if I didn't need it, and somehow the tension was gone. Most of our children's irritating behavior, as well as their charming ways, last only for a season—unless we make a big deal about it. This is why we should record the good and ignore the bad and the ugly.

My journal can't take all the credit for solving this problem. My husband had the brilliant idea to let each of the kids choose a section of the garden to be their own, so they could take some pride in their work. The kids all loved this idea—especially when we took them to the nursery and let them pick out their own plants.

William Zinsser offers some advice on solving writing problems that seems to me applicable to parenting problems as well. "All writing boils down to a succession of big and small decisions," he says—and this is certainly true of parenting. "No decision is too small to be worth wrestling with, . . . and every writing problem contains within itself the decision that will solve it."[41] Writing about problems in your personal journal will help you analyze them more objectively. What are the decisions that must be made? What choices do you have? How can you determine the best one?

Writing Can Alert You to Deeper Insights

Here's an entry from Britta's book dated 7/22/93. She was two and a half.

> You came toddling into the kitchen—rubbing your eyes, dragging blanket and rabbit—pleading up at me with a sad, silent face.
> Oh, little one, bad dream?
> We sat in the rocking chair and sang together your favorite song The "I love you" song (from Barney):
>
> When I tucked you in and sang another little song, you reached to hold my hand, opened your eyes and said, "You are my mommy," then turned your head and fell asleep.

---

[41] From the Introduction to *On Writing Well.*

How those words melted my heart! I've gotten a double benefit from this entry: a happy memory and a helpful insight. One day, as I was pondering something that was troubling me, I felt inspired to call a particular friend. So I dropped what I was doing and picked up the phone. It was one of those conversations that just melt trouble away. When I hung up the phone, I wanted to thank God for the gift of my friend and her words, so I stood in the kitchen, looked up, and said, "You are my God," I felt my heavenly Father's smile. I learned how to do that from my daughter—and from my journal to her. Receiving her love taught me how to show love.

Making the World a Better Place, One Word at a Time

Julie Cameron has written a number of books that inspire writers. In one, called *The Right to Write*, her introduction includes these words:

> I have a fantasy. It's the pearly gates. St. Peter has out his questionnaire, he asks me the Big Question, "What did you do that we should let you in?"
> "I convinced people they should write,'" I tell him. The great gates swing open.[42]

Of course she's being facetious. But her point is that writing is a good thing, and if more people did it, the world would be a better place. I believe writing for our children is a very good thing, and if we do even a little of it, we're making our families, and therefore the world, better.

---

[42] Julia Cameron, *The Right to Write: An Invitation to the Writing Life* (New York: Putnam, 1998), xvii.

Coat of Many Colors

My children walk out the door,
And the world is very big.
But they are warm and bright,
Each dressed in the many-colored coat
I've woven with letters of love
On the backing of bound pages.

Appendix

Books to Read with Children

> *No book is really worth reading at the age of ten*
> *which is not equally (and often more) worth reading*
> *at the age of fifty and beyond.*
>
> —C. S. Lewis

An Important Habit to Establish

One of the most pleasurable tasks of parenting is teaching our children (through modeling and direct experience) that, generally speaking, the best way to end the day is by relaxing for a few minutes with a good book. Many evenings we get home late from activities and it is impossible to read, but on nights we are home, reading is a priority. The books listed here have made it easy for me to make time for reading because all of them are as entertaining as they are educational. When such a delicious treat awaits, it's easy for both parent and child to put away work, turn off all interruptors (including the telephone), and enter together the world of a good book.

Sometimes we make tea for reading time. And I provide sketchbooks for the children to draw in, but I don't let them do homework or play on the computer while I read.

If you have children who are at different levels of understanding, you may have to read them separate books. I never have time to read more than one book on any given evening, so I read one book to one child. The others are free to listen. Right now I have a different book going with each of the three kids, and a fourth that my husband and I are reading together when we can find time. Sometimes I read aloud while he drives.

Here are ten books (one is a set of books) that I've read with our kids and that have enriched me as much as they have the children.

Bahn, Mary, *The Memory Box* (Morton Grove, IL: Albert Whitman and Company, 1992).

Ages 6–11. My son's teacher read this to him in fourth grade, and he came home excited about it. We found the book at the local library and read it as a family. It's about a grandfather who realizes he has Alzheimer's disease and starts a memory box with his grandson to preserve the memories of times they have shared. Jack (my son) decided that since I write a journal for him, he could keep a memory box with Dad. In it they'll keep souvenirs from fishing trips and sporting events and other things they do together.

The book made us cry. What a tragedy to think of losing one's memory. I think the message that Alzheimer's disease says to the world is that memory is precious and not to be taken for granted.

Clements, Andrew, *The Landry News* (New York: Aladdin/ Simon & Schuster, 2000).

Ages 8–12. My favorite scene is when the girl comes home from school discouraged about a problem she's facing. Her mom (the two of them live alone) happens to be sitting on her bed reading her Bible. She shares with her daughter that God wants us to "speak the truth in love." The rest of the book illustrates the practical way in which the girl learns to live out this command.

Creech, Sharon, *Love That Dog* (New York: HarperCollins, 2001).

Ages 8–12, especially boys who don't think they like poetry. This is the story of how a boy's love for his dog opened up the world of poetry to him. The appendix includes the eight poems used by the boy's teacher for an amazingly effective poetry unit. Jack and I read this book together when he was eight or nine. He completely identified with the main character (whose name also happens to be Jack).

Eliot, George, *Silas Marner* (New York: Knopf, 1993).

Ages 15 and up. Here is a powerful story of redemption. Betsy and I were very moved by it. But the sentence structure and vocabulary are 150 years out of date, so it's a brain-stretcher. We read it aloud, and I frequently needed to paraphrase or explain things. We kept a dictionary nearby as well. This sort of challenging reading is important for high school students, of course, and prepares them for independent reading of the classics. This little book is the perfect introduction to the classics because it has a fairy-tale element that kids recognize and respond to. This short novel might spark long discussions on big questions such as, Why do Christians hurt each other? How could God let the church destroy an innocent believer? The moral lessons here are clear. We see how teenagers who don't control their impulses ruin their own lives and the lives of others. And we see how love can heal a broken life. Keep the Kleenex handy.

Helprin, Mark, *A City in Winter* (New York: Viking Ariel/ Penguin), illustrated by Chris Van Allsburg.

Ages 8 and above. Stunning illustrations. Beautiful prose. This book is a treat. The story deals will the grand themes of identity, destiny, preparation, patience, and purpose.

Lewis, C. S., *Chronicles of Narnia*—all seven books in the series (New York: HarperCollins).

Ages 8 and up. These seven books are ideal for family reading because they are packed with multiple layers of meaning. Children who are too young to read them independently can grasp much by listening. They love the believable animal characters. Older kids relish the adventure and the brilliantly constructed fantasy world of Narnia (on the order of Tolkein's Middle Earth, though not as detailed). The main characters of this series travel back and forth from our world to Narnia (and beyond). Adults appreciate the rich insights about life and relationships.

MacDonald, George, *At the Back of the North Wind* (New York: Children's Classics/Dilithium Press, Ltd., 1990), Illustrated by Jessie Wilcox Smith. (Also available as a Puffin Classics paperback.)

All ages (listening). This was the first George MacDonald book I ever read. I saw the beautiful book on a sale table and snatched it up. We started it as a family read-aloud book, but we soon lost Greg and the girls; the writing style is archaic and the plot is sometimes slow. But my soul was stirred by the amazing bursts of light that flash out of the story from time to time. Jack was still a preschooler at the time—happy just to have me sit with him and read any book—so he stuck with me. Much of the book was too deep for him to grasp, but he could tell that I loved the story and the characters and the author. He shared this love. About five years later, when Jack was home from school sick, we read some chapters from the book again and loved them even more.

MacDonald, George, *The Princess and Curdie* (London: Penguin, 1994.)
All ages (listening). This is the sequel to *The Princess and the Goblin.*

MacDonald, George, *The Princess and the Goblin* (New York: Knopf, 1993). First published in 1871.
All ages (listening). Here are spiritual truths told in fairy-tale form. Deep insights about God and reality and the highest way to live are easy to digest because they are wrapped in such a delightful story. You'll profit from wisdom that will be too deep for your children to grasp; they'll latch on to the story. Both adults and children come away from any George MacDonald book with a stronger capacity to recognize and to love goodness.

Taylor, Helen L., *Little Pilgrim's Progress,* adapted from John Bunyan's classic work. (Chicago: Moody Press, year).
All ages (listening). Ages 10–12 (independent reading). Short chapters (three pages) are perfect for bedtime reading. I found this version more enjoyable than the adult version. I've never had the courage to attempt the original. Even the modern revised edition required a lot of work. I spent half my time looking up footnotes. This children's version, on the other hand, was good devotional material for me.
The great thing about *Pilgrim's Progress* is that it shapes our thinking to understand life as a journey. The various difficulties along the way are put into perspective as simply being challenges to overcome so we can move on.

To order additional copies of

Love Letters To a Child

call toll free: (877) 421-READ (7323)

or order online at: www.winepressbooks.com

You can contact the author at
traceyfinck@msn.com